BE THE LIME

...The World Has Enough Lemons.

FRED M. REWEY

First Printing, 2016

ISBN-13: 978-0692800034
ISBN-10: 0692800034

Exposure One
13900 County Road 455
Suite 107-252
Clermont, FL 34711

Ordering Information:

Quantity sales. Special discounts are available on quantity purchases by corporations, associations, and others. For details, contact the publisher at the address above.

Orders by U.S. trade bookstores and wholesalers

www.BeTheLime.com

Printed in the United States of America

About The Author...

Ugh, the author bio page. You know, where some "guest" says really impressive things about the author.

The writer, in third person voice of course, is supposed to say really cool things about themselves, about their company and their brand.

Here is the deal.

I help people stand out.

I say, "*Be The Lime Because The World Has Enough Lemons.*"

It is not hard to stand out. It is not hard to do things differently. Most people just can't see the forest through the trees.

Finding that one thing. That one unique angle that raises the bar for everyone else and propels you to the top is the fun part.

After countless requests from my clients, friends,

and the guy that sells me pizza, I decided to make some of these strategies public.

You may or may not know me...but I guarantee you have seen my work.

Who I am matters, but not as much as you getting real results. You know, the kind you can measure! But, since this is the bio page, here are a few tidbits about me.

I enjoy writing, traveling, motorcycling, and flying stunt planes. I have built and sold companies; not because selling was the goal, but because it was fun to turn a hobby into a business.

I am a total foodie and wish people would stop posting recipes online *(I feel like I need to make them all)*.

I am pretty sure you won't beat me in a game of air hockey but you could probably take me in game of bowling without a problem.

I could talk for hours and hours about marketing and love sharing the things I find out.

I want to thank you for picking up the book. I hope you like it and, even more, I hope you put it to good use!

Whether you, your business, or your brand is getting lost in all the 'noise' out there, I will help you **BE THE LIME**.

- Fred Rewey

Table of Contents

Introduction

> *"If you'll not settle for anything less than your best, you will be amazed at what you can accomplish in your lives."*
>
> – Vince Lombardi

Let's face it. The game has changed.

Yellow pages are now used as doorstops. Billboards are passed unnoticed. Newspapers and magazines can't drop print versions fast enough in favor of online e-letters and websites – if even staying in business at all.

For some people, it has never been more challenging for businesses to get the attention of (new) local consumers and build a brand.

Today's savvy businessperson knows one thing for sure:

"Your business and your brand starts online."

The average consumer searches online for whatever

they need long before stepping into a store. That means if you don't have a strong online presence, your offline brick and mortar store will suffer...severely.

But, there is good news.

It is not difficult to get the attention of your local consumers. It is also not difficult to do it with little or no money. It is not even very challenging to get ahead of most of your competition.

You know why?

Most of your competitors suck at marketing.

There is an old joke:

Two hikers round a corner and come face to face with an enormous bear that rises up on its haunches and roars at them.

The first hiker sits down and starts to swap out his hiking boots for a pair of tennis shoes.

"What are you doing? Shoes are not going to help you outrun a bear," the second hiker says.

The first hiker replies, "I don't need to outrun the bear, I just need to outrun you."

The same is true in winning the hearts, minds, and money of local customers.

In the end, when it comes to marketing, you only need to do better than your competition. And most of your competition is doing everything wrong.

You might think that your competition is doing great.

You see them rank higher than you on an Internet search. You might see them with all the latest marketing techniques, seemingly "crushing it."

What you might not see is a whole lot of money being spent in desperation to find business. Money they will never get back. Money that is wasted.

And maybe, just maybe, they **do** have a clue.

Maybe they have learned, through trial and error, a way to increase their business.

Maybe they have hired someone who knows what they are doing.

Maybe they have read this book.

So, what if you are dealing with someone that does have a great online presence and the lion's share of the local market?

It is time to take that back!

We consult with businesses and brands every week. Both big and small, they are all faced with the same challenge as you may be facing right now and, oftentimes, the solutions are just a few action items that make all the difference.

Who is this book for?

- ✓ I have written this book for the local businessperson with a brick and mortar that needs an edge.

- ✓ I have written this book for anyone who is trying to sell or build a brand exclusively online.

- ✓ I have written this book for anyone who is trying to get more exposure for their brand.

- ✓ I have written this book for anyone who feels like it is "too late" to get in on the game and succeed.

Most of these strategies can be expanded to take your business global or simply cultivate your own backyard.

In this book, I am going to walk you through the maze of Internet marketing choices and focus on the ones that can help your bottom line.

I want to bring attention to those strategies that are easy to implement and will have the greatest impact on your business. I am also going to suggest some areas to avoid (either due to cost, effectiveness, or time).

I understand time and budget.

I understand what it takes to run a business.

I understand that you have a business to run.

Wearing a full-time online marketing hat was probably not in your plan. I get it.

I am going to show you how to get the most use out of your time spent online – and get you back to work!

If you are like most business owners, you probably have a couple questions, right now, that you want answered.

Each chapter in this book is its own lesson.

In the beginning we will focus on some core beliefs at the 30,000 foot level. Call them "tips" or "strategies." They will make sure we are on the same page before we tackle a variety of ways for you to make an impact.

At the end of some chapters you will find "Action Items;" use those to create a plan. Think of it as a "to do" list. You don't need to do them all. Just implementing *some* items will make a big difference that you can see immediately.

Be sure to read the chapters that have topics you know absolutely nothing about. Those just might be your biggest moneymakers!

So, let's get started on separating you and your brand from the lemons of the world.

Be the Lime – the world has enough lemons.

BE THE LIME

Chapter One:

FINDING YOUR INNER LIME.

"Sometimes I Pretend to be Normal.
But it Gets Boring.
So I Go Back to Being Me."

- unknown

Before we get too deep into the things that make Limes, well, Limes, you might be thinking to yourself, "What makes ME a lime?"

Frankly, that is great question.

No two limes are alike and finding **your** inner lime does require some work. Don't get me wrong, it's not like building a rocket or trying to not cry out when you step on a Lego.

Nope. I just need to help you find your way.

Let me let you in on a little secret.

There is only ONE hurdle in being a Lime. The rest is just, well, execution.

Ready for it? Here you go:

Finding your own voice.

Once you find your own voice the rest becomes pretty easy.

So what do I mean by finding your own voice? *Seems pretty sketchy huh?*

I have worked at a ton of different jobs in my life and built several businesses. Some people call it "entrepreneurial" but the fact of the matter is that I have always looked at it as I had a short attention span. I just like to try and experience new things. Along the way there have been some great successes. But I never knew why.

Several of the jobs I have worked, I loved and felt like 'myself,' and others, well, I just put on a face and acted my way through it.

When online businesses started emerging I was able to write more. I really enjoy writing. And shooting videos.

I know, it is not for everyone, but for me it is a great way to get stuff out of my head, even if no one reads or watches it. Luckily for me, and contrary to repeated lectures from my 4th grade teacher, everyone can find an audience who will listen!

Over the years I have found a common denominator to successfully marketing a brand or product.

You have to be yourself. You have to have your own voice.

Now, before you skip to another chapter or think I am going to start pitching you on *hot-yogurt-meditation,** let me say that most people *think* they are being themselves and *they are not*.

Pretty sure there is no such thing as 'hot-yogurt-meditation,' but all bets are off and I am too afraid to search it out on the Internet to be sure.

Finding your own voice is very much like having an opinion.

It's like cats and dogs.

Imagine being at a cocktail party *(does anyone use*

that term anymore?) where you don't know anyone. All you do know is that half of the people like cats and half of the people like dogs.

The dog people *hate* cats and the cat people *hate* dogs.

Now, you personally, are a bird person, but you are going to engage in conversation nonetheless.

Most people will walk that fine line of trying to make everyone happy, without internally sacrificing the other group, even if they aren't currently included in the conversation.

In other words, most people will say to a cat person, "They look nice. I have seen lots of videos on Facebook of them. They seem fluffy."

And, when talking to a dog person they will say, "They look nice. I have seen lots of them at the park. They seem to have a lot of fur."

At the end of the night, no one will remember you. You are not on the same page with either group. You were neutral and neutral is boring.

Frankly, if you wanted to be a lime, you would have been better off saying you *hated* both cats and dogs. At least if you did that, two things would happen:

1. Everyone at this party would remember you…and tell their friends.

2. Other groups will invite you to their party; people you didn't even know about, because they share the same view.

16

Now, I am not saying pretend to hate them both. I am just saying if that is who you are, go with it.

I use to write to cast a big net. You know, try and make everyone happy.

The end result is that, although some people will follow you, none of them are super passionate about you.

When I adopted more of a Richard Branson, "Screw it, Let's Do it" attitude, it got a lot easier and I started to get raving fans.

So, in a nutshell, let me say this about finding your voice.

You are going to piss off some people.

Someone once told me that they can break up their fans and non-fans into three groups:

- People that *like* you.
- People that want to *be* you.
- People that *dislike* you.

Now "dislike" might be a strong word, but it is not far off. You are NOT going to make everyone happy. **So don't try**.

Once you have your voice, like I said, the rest is just execution.

Remember, you don't need to (and shouldn't) do everything. You don't need to play in every social media outlet that comes along. I certainly don't.

There are numerous ways to express yourself now. This might surprise you, but some of these methods might even seem a bit scary to you now, but trust me, you will get there.

- ✓ You can be in front of the camera and create videos.
- ✓ You can be behind the camera and use a Power Point or Screen Capture.
- ✓ You can share stories.
- ✓ You can write news.
- ✓ You can share recipes.
- ✓ You can share photos.
- ✓ You can share humor.
- ✓ You can do **ANYTHING** and find an audience.

If any of those things seem impossible or outside your comfort zone, just wait. I promise you will get there when we find the right path for you!

But that is amazing part about being you. NO ONE else can do it!

I love the quote, "Be yourself; everyone else is taken" by Oscar Wilde

Why be nervous about being yourself?

We get nervous about shooting a video or writing a post when we are trying hard to *be someone else.*

When we are ourselves, the words come out pretty easy.

If you are already a Lime, then you know what I am talking about. You can use this book to tweak and grow your audience, build your business, increase your brand awareness.

If you are not there yet, I am positive you will get there a lot sooner than you think.

The world has enough lemons. Be you. Be the Lime.

BE THE LIME

Chapter Two:

CLONING YOURSELF IN THREE EASY STEPS!

---

*"Oh good, just what we needed.
More rabbits."*

– Unknown scientist on
perfectly cloning rabbits.

Let me tell you a secret: I am generally pretty lazy.

It seems every motivational quote that shows up on my Facebook wall lately is talking about how you should never take short cuts.

Of course, it is not just the words. That would be insulting enough. Nope, the quotes come with a fuzzy bunny, a dramatic sunset, or some mountain climber hanging off the side of a cliff with one hand.

"There are no shortcuts to
any place worth going"

– Beverly Sills

"There are no shortcuts in life
– only those we imagine."

– Frank Leahy

"If you take shortcuts,
you get cut short."

– Gary Busey

Really? Even Gary Busey is weighing in on this subject? I am going to have to call B.S.!

My coffee maker made the coffee this morning. You know, instead of over an open fire made of sticks. *Is that a short cut?*

I am flying to Texas tomorrow for some events but I will be taking a plane instead of riding a horse in a wagon train. Is *that* a short cut?

Let's face it, you don't want this brand or business promotion to be your full time job. Shortcuts are fine, just make sure you end up in the same place and deliver the same quality.

Three things right out of the gate are going to save you time and headaches!

Outsourcing, **Leveraging**, and **Tools**.

Let me briefly tackle them in order...

Outsourcing

You may think outsourcing is outside your budget.

In my *Be the Lime Monthly Membership* I teach people how to do it themselves, in the least amount of time as possible. Its inexpensive and measurable.

That said, there a lot of things you can outsource that don't cost very much so there is no need to do them yourself!

There are a multitude of sites online that offer services but I do want to mention two here.

Fiverr.com and
UpWork.com *(previously Elance)*.

As the name would imply, most of the items that you hire for on Fiverr.com cost, yep, $5.00. I use

Fiverr.com for a lot of quick things...

- ✓ Logo creation
- ✓ Converting something to PSD
- ✓ Converting something to Vector
- ✓ One-off Video Editing
- ✓ Cleaning up sound on a recording
- ✓ And much more.

UpWork.com is more a "bid" model. You submit your project and let people, from all around the world, bid for your work. I use Upwork.com for things like...

- ✓ Creating Book Covers
- ✓ Editing Articles
- ✓ Editing Books
- ✓ Graphic Design
- ✓ Film Logos
- ✓ Video Production
- ✓ Transcription

With both Fiverr.com and UpWork.com you can review the user ratings of the people you are considering– for added peace of mind, before hiring.

Leveraging

Leveraging is something that I could spend another 100 pages on. But I do want to say this:

One action can equal multiple results.

We can't clone ourselves, but we can clone and split apart our materials.

Let's say you do a 10-minute video on your product or brand.

I am going to call it **"5 Tricks to Teach Your Pet Frog."**

Maybe you did the video on Facebook live (and recorded it). Maybe you simply just shot it on your iPhone.

Whatever the case, you now have 10 minutes of video to share.

Here are a few things you could do with it.

1. Share the video on your Facebook fan page (in full)

2. Share the video on your website (in full)

3. Share the video on YouTube (in full)

4. Break the video into 5 pieces (one video for each 'trick').
   a. Share on Twitter (x5)
   b. Share on Instagram Stories (x5)
   c. Share on Facebook (x5)
   d. Share on YouTube (x5)

5. Create 7-10 Quote Pictures from the video that can be shared on...
   a. Instagram (x7)
   b. Pinterest (x7)
   c. Twitter (x7)
   d. Facebook (x7)

6. Strip out the audio and create…
    a. Podcast

Ok, you get the idea.

One action, shooting a 10 min video now, equals a heck of a lot of "posts" going forward.

You could either do all the stuff above or simply shoot the video and outsource someone to do all the rest!

Tools

You can go to BeTheLime.com/Resources and check out some of my latest favorite online tools for Limes but I do want to mention a couple examples here.

Need to create a Quote Post?

Pictures with quotes are worth gold in social media. People share, like, and comment all time, and that is good for you!

You can certainly outsource this function, but there are some great apps out there that go right on your phone.

Word Swag is one of my favorites right now (*Canva is another good one*). I can search a specific subject and Word Swag gives me license free photos to choose from (or I can use my own photo).

Then I get to choose from a multitude of fonts and styles. Very professional looking quote photos in just a few minutes.

Going on vacation? Schedule your content!

Ok, even if you are NOT going on vacation you are going to want get to know the likes of Hootsuite and Buffer.

Both of these programs (and there are others out there) will enable you to "schedule" your Facebook posts, Twitter Tweets, etc. in a main dash board.

I do this all the time.

I find something interesting and schedule it out for some time later. My daily posts are a mix of posts that I have done "live" in real-time and others that have been long-ago scheduled.

Both these tools have great reporting that will let you know the best times to post – to get the most response.

Action Items.

You know, the kind of thing Limes work on:

- Check out Fiverr.com and Upwork.com. What items could you outsource?

- What can you leverage? A Video? A recording? Can you share a picture on more than one social media platform (hint: Yes, you can!).

- Check out Hootsuite and Buffer

- Download Word Swag and check out Canva for picture quotes (you will thank me later)

- Check out BeTheLime.com/Resources for some additional info.

Chapter Three:

YOU WILL NEVER BE 100% READY...AND THAT IS OK!

"Imperfect action is better than perfect inaction."

– Harry Truman

You might be the kind of person that is pretty much skipping over the quotes at the top of each chapter.

I don't blame you.

I mean really, who cares what the author of the book threw at the top of each chapter to fill space, make him/her look well read, or some veiled attempt at inferred credibility.

But this one is worth repeating...

"Imperfect action is better than perfect inaction."

– Harry Truman

Now I am not really sure Harry Truman said that. I mean the **INTERNET** says he did...so...at some point it will become fact. But whoever said it was spot-on.

I have seen numerous clients with awesome ideas that never get off the ground because they are so obsessed with making whatever they are building 'perfect.'

They needed ALL their ducks in a row before moving forward.

There is a difference between 'perfection' and 'prolonging.'

I think you should try and be *prepared* for whatever you are doing. Perfection may just have to come later.

For example, if you are launching an email campaign, then it is good to make sure you have items in place to track the results. This is also the point where I speak with clients about A/B testing some email subject lines.

At the very basic level this is simply sending out two different subject lines. Half the group gets one subject line and the other half gets another.

Group A Subject Line: This is going fast!

Group B Subject Line: Don't get left out.

Let's just say that I divide my database into two. 50% are in group A and 50% are in group B.

The goal is simply to see which group opens more emails.

Pro Tip: Believe it or not, the subject line of your email can make a huge difference in how many people read versus delete it without reading.

Now, to A/B test it does not take a lot of work. Most email services can do this for you (or you can find a workaround that gives you the same affect).

Herein lies the problem.

I tell someone who has yet to send ANY emails

about A/B testing and I create another reason for them to delay in taking action.

They think, "Man, that is a great idea. I need to make sure I A/B test my subject lines. I am going to wait until I get that set up before I send out any emails."

And then more and more time goes by and the person never sends *any* emails.

It would have been FAR BETTER for the person to send out one email, not A/B tested, and even picked a pretty cruddy subject line, than do nothing at all.

At least that is an ACTION. You can always tweak from there.

You would be surprised how many of us, myself included, have this problem...

...and some of us don't even know we are doing it!

In software development it is called 'Feature Creep.'

A company is all excited about releasing some new computer software and they bring in some focus groups and beta testers.

As with all outside opinions, you will be hit with both good and bad recommendations.

Let's say the beta testers have some great ideas for some improvements.

You decide to delay your release a week or so to make those changes.

Then someone comes up with another idea...and it is a great one. But, it will delay the launch another month.

You have to decide is it worth it to delay or are you better off launching today and saying something to the effect of "Hey, these additional features are coming soon!"

When we are close to a brand or project we want to put our best foot forward...and I think we should.

But not to the point of inaction.

I go through this thought process weekly and here is one method that helps me.

I have to answer two questions.

1. Will doing (or not doing) this action PREVENT a sale or my brand from moving forward?
2. Will doing (or not doing) this action make someone unhappy with their purchase (ie: refund)?

These two questions are paramount in helping me decide whether or not my energy needs to be spend on a particular area.

If it will not affect sales, and it won't make anyone unhappy with their purchase, it is not my highest priority. I may get to it in my "spare time" but not right now.

As entrepreneurs, we have a million things in our brains we want to do. But there is also not enough time in the day.

It's never perfect.

Once you realize that your brand or project will never be 100% complete-to-your-liking, it will never be 100% perfect, you can give yourself permission to go out there and DO things.

Doing will always trump not doing.

Action Items.

You know, the kind of thing Limes work on:

- Do Something...

- ...Now

Chapter Four:

AVATARS - UNDERSTANDING YOUR AUDIENCE

"Sometimes your whole life boils down to one insane move.

- Jake Sully, Avatar

Before you skip this chapter and think it is a review for James Cameron's award winning movie, hang with me for a minute. This chapter will be your key start to just about everything when it comes to selling a product (or yourself) on social media.

Let me first start by saying that although the Avatar process has been around for a very long time, it is one that I personally, and foolishly, neglected in my early years.

I often skipped this step thinking I had a full understanding of my target market and how to market to them.

That was my first mistake. I was definitely not acting like a Lime...I was acting like a Lemon. Ugh.

I was marketing in a broad sense, from a 30,000-foot level, and never, really, speaking to one person at a time.

Whether you're selling something or just trying to increase your own social media, you must connect with people. The Avatar process will help you better target that communication.

It is the process of understanding *who* your customer is and *how* they think.

What motivates them? What do they like? Dislike? How old are they? What is their income level?

This person or "Avatar" is a makeup of your ideal customer.

36

The closer we get to understanding this person, the better our sales, the more followers we have, and the better our retention and relevance.

I look for four areas when building my ideal Avatar. Although the emphasis on each category may vary from client to client, the essence is always the same.

What you need to know about your ideal client or avatar...

- What are their Values and Goals?
- Where do they get their Information about the world?
- What are their fears and challenges?
- What are their objections (if I am selling something)?

Limes know their audience beyond a doubt. Down to a seemingly "over doing it" level – but, it pays off.

Let's take a look at a case study.

This is an example of an Avatar for a brand that sells products online (via a website). This is the make-up of their audience – how they think, what they believe in.

Question One: What are their Values and Goals?

Values:
- ✓ Willing to continue to learn
- ✓ Desire to keep in the forefront of trends
- ✓ Family and Friends
- ✓ Uses 'best practices' (not looking for

sketchy gray area shortcuts)
- ✓ Pride in their business

Goals:

- ✓ Trying to increase business
- ✓ Self-employed
- ✓ Take more time off
- ✓ Sells digital products through websites (or wishes to)
- ✓ Desire for stronger social media presence

Question Two: Where do they get Information about the world?

- ✓ Facebook
- ✓ Twitter
- ✓ Fast Company Magazine
- ✓ The Late Show
- ✓ The Daily Skimm

Question Three: What are their fears and challenges?

Challenges:

- ✓ Not enough hours in the day
- ✓ Too many 'programs' out there to learn from.
- ✓ No game plan
- ✓ Staying focused (jumping from shiny object to shiny object)
- ✓ Assumptions based on inaccurate information

Fears:

- ✓ Business Failing
- ✓ Having to go back and work for someone else

- ✓ Inner Critic
- ✓ Wasting Time
- ✓ Making the wrong choice

*Question Four: **What are their objections (if I am selling something)?***

- ✓ Will this really work?
- ✓ Will I have time to go through all this?
- ✓ Will I even use the information?
- ✓ Will I make my money back?
- ✓ Is there ongoing support?

Depending on what we are selling we will also include some basic demographic info...

- ✓ Male/Female
- ✓ Age
- ✓ Married or Single
- ✓ Location
- ✓ Annual Income
- ✓ Level of Education

Now we can communicate with them!

With a complete avatar created, we can begin to see how important this will be when it comes to marketing ourselves and our products.

Mostly likely, we will tweak our Avatar over time as new people enter the picture, but this gives us a solid start.

Let's say I was trying to sell this person on a **Be the Lime Monthly Membership**.

I could start with any number of pointsand any of which could be the basis of an advertisement on Facebook, a social media post, or a blog article.

"Not enough hours in the day" – Be The Lime monthly members get easy to implement strategies they can use in minutes, not days.

"Will I make my money back?" – Any one strategy learned in the Be The Lime Monthly Membership can turn into real income you can measure right away.

"I want to use 'best practices' (not looking for sketchy gray area shortcuts)" – Be the Lime will NEVER cut corners that put you on 'black lists' or get you in deep water with your providers. We don't believe in SPAM or black hat methods of marketing.

But maybe our Avatar isn't for Be the Lime clients. Maybe it is for another, completely different business.

Let's pretend a completely different business *just happens* to have the same Avatar.

What about a Cleaning Service?

If I am trying to sell a cleaning service to someone, and I took a look at my avatar, I would start with:

"Not enough hours in the day" - *This person is busy. I can give them back time by offering my cleaning services.*

"Value Family and Friends" – I suspect they don't want their friends and family to see a dirty house. An

advertisement with a before and after picture would speak volumes.

What about something as simple as a Coffee Shop, again with the same Avatar?

"Pride in their business" – Just like you, we have pride in our business and our reputation. Maybe the coffee shop is "family friendly" as well.

In reality, if I did have a cleaning service or coffee shop we would have created a completely different Avatar.

Now, it is your turn.

Who is YOUR Audience? Are you selling a product or just looking for greater personal branding? In either case, you need an Avatar.

Question One: What are their Values and Goals?

Values:

    1. _____

    2. _____

    3. _____

    4. _____

    5. _____

Goals:

    1. _____

    2. _____

    3. _____

    4. _____

    5. _____

Question Two: Where do they get Information about the world?

     1. _____
     2. _____
     3. _____
     4. _____
     5. _____

Question Three: What are their fears and challenges?

Challenges:
     1. _____
     2. _____
     3. _____
     4. _____
     5. _____
Fears:
     1. _____
     2. _____
     3. _____
     4. _____
     5. _____

Question Four: What are their objections (if I am selling something)?

     1. _____
     2. _____
     3. _____
     4. _____
     5. _____

Depending on what we are selling we will also include some basic demographic info...

Male/Female:
Age:
Married or Single:
Location:
Annual Income:
Level of Education:

Action Items.

You know, the kind of thing Limes work on:

- Fill out the above Avatar for your business or brand.

- Do you see any insight to their method of thinking and how what you say or share will speak directly to them?

- Check out <u>BeTheLime.com</u> for an Avatar Cheat Sheet!

Chapter Five:

DOUBLE DOWN ON YOUR STRENGTHS, NOT YOUR WEAKNESSES.

"Trent, I'm telling you baby,
you always double down on 11."

– Swingers

When working with new clients, this just may be the hardest concept to convince people of.

Alright Limes, remember this phrase.

"Double down on your strengths, not your weaknesses."

Why is this so important?

Anytime you hire a traditional marketing or branding consultant, they are going to come in and do some sort of research.

Typically, that research involves talking to your customers and seeing what they like and hate most about your brand in the form of focus groups and surveys.

Let's say we do a focus group with Honda and Lamborghini.

If we ask the Honda group what they like about Honda cars, the group is going to focus on things like it is practical, affordable and reliable.

If we had the Honda group explain what they don't like (or would like to see more of) they might respond with "faster, sportier, or sexier."

Honda is a practical car, but not necessarily the one you wanted to pick up, and impress, your prom date in.

Any conversation about a Honda will typically turn to 'gas mileage' not '0-60 track speed.'

Your typical "expert" brand consultant will come to the review meeting, throw the results into a power point, and suggest that Honda change their marketing to make up for their deficiencies.

They will throw around really cool terms like "untapped market" and "progressive growth opportunity."

The fact of the matter is that this is VERY dangerous to the brand.

The only way a massive change in marketing direction is successful is if the TARGET market is ultimately greater (in numbers or sales volume) than your original core audience.

If Honda was to take that advice and start changing their commercials they would ultimately lose their core audience.

The person looking to upgrade their "practical" Honda would turn away from commercials that make it look like a crazy impulse buy.

They WANT to be practical. That is why they had the Honda in the first place.

The opposite holds true for Lamborghini.

They certainly are not hitting any 'affordability' marks in their advertising and not pushing anything related to reliability (even though the car may or may not be just as reliable as a Honda).

They don't because we have been trained to believe their cars are flat out fast, sexy and scream "success."

You are going to get that date with a blond or make your co-workers green with envy because you drive a car that goes fast and turns heads. *

Let's face it, those ads are sexist for a reason; they work on certain market segments.

What if Lamborghini did go after Honda's "practical and sensible" audience?

A Big, Fat, Fail.

Who (or is it "whom") of the people that currently purchase a Lamborghini are going to want to be seen in one if it represents playing it safe and being practical?

Lamborghini would lose their core market almost overnight.

Both companies need to play to their strengths.

Another example is that until recently, McDonald's was in a free fall spin downward.

They were losing to 'craft' burger places opening up everywhere, health conscience people, and general complacency.

McDonald's saw this and reacted with their first of many mistakes.

They lost sight of their core audience; ditched the "super-sized" items and proceeded to go down the road of creating a healthy menu.

Consumers had no clue "what" McDonald's was at that point and I am going to guess that McDonalds no longer had a solid Avatar about who their customer was.

Sure, they did a good job marketing their coffee, but what if I wanted to eat?

I wasn't in the market for a McSalad when I knew Panera was awesome at making fresh salads. I just pictured McDonald's, a BURGER place, using the same lettuce they put on the burgers to make my Cobb Salad. Blech!

Panera does not do burgers and McDonald's should not bother with salads.

Recently McDonald's got some good advice and it had nothing to do with expanding their menu, roping in a new audience, or focusing on their weaknesses.

They doubled down on their strengths!

They added "all-day breakfast" and it was a HUGE hit.

This only needed them to win back their existing audience, and it did, in a BIG way!

With a million lunch options but very few breakfast options, McDonald's tapped into a market that wanted an Egg McMuffin after 10:30 am., and it brought back customers in droves.

I am NOT saying IGNORE your weaknesses.

I am NOT suggesting that you ignore what you are not good at or what segments of the market you are not hitting.

I am saying, DO NOT SACRIFICE YOUR CORE MARKET to try and gain another.

Double Down on Your Strengths, not your weaknesses.

Action Items.
You know, the kind of thing Limes work on:

- Make a list of your strengths. What is unique to you or your brand?

- Make a list of your weaknesses (or market segments you do not have).

- If you were to go after, or improve, your weaknesses would it take away from the market that you have in your strengths? If so…rethink that.

- If you doubled down on the strong part of your brand, would you pick up even more clients?

Chapter Six:

THE LIFETIME VALUE OF A CUSTOMER

"Make a customer, not a sale."

~ Katherine Barchetti

When conversations turn to marketing, especially via the Internet, the letters ROI are not far behind.

ROI (Return on Investment) is at the forefront of everyone's mind. It is also why some brands and business have not moved forward with online marketing; because they don't know how to quantify the cost.

How much should you pay for a lead? How much should you pay for a sale?

*I have to say, without a shadow of a doubt, people make this **far** too complex.*

Let's start with a brick and mortar business. And let's say you have a shop that sells fancy cookies.*

*I don't know what constitutes 'fancy' cookies, maybe limes added, but I am hungry as I write this...so just go with it.

You make amazing cookies with amazing ingredients. The cookies are great, and the presentation is also stunning. This often leads to a customer giving them away as gifts as well as buying them for themselves.

Say you are going to advertise on Facebook. And without going into any additional targeting for this example, let's say you focus on a 15-mile radius for now.

Fact 1 - You know that when someone tries your cookies they tend to spend $15 per month. You also know that same person will spend, on average, $75 over the next 4 months giving cookies as gifts.

Fact 2 - That means your customer in the next four months will spend $60 on themselves and $75 on others for a total of $135.00.

Now, let's say you run a Facebook ad.

100 people clicked on your ad and, to keep the numbers simple, let's say that cost you $1 per click.

You spent $100 for 100 people to click your ad and come to your site.

Of those 100 people, you know for certain that 5 became customers.

You paid $20 per customer ($100 in ads to end up with 5 customers).

Each customer is going to spend $135.00 in the next four months (on average).

So, as long as the marketing stays the same, for every $20 you spend on the ad, you will earn $115.00 ($135 - $20).

That is pretty easy on the short term but what about the long term?

What if I said it cost you $135 to obtain the same customer? Is it worth it?

That really depends on two things.

1. Will that customer bring in other customers just by sharing the cookies *and*

2. What is lifetime value (revenue) of the customer?

We said in the first four months the person spends $135 total. But what do they spend after that?

If they spend nothing than the 'lifetime value' of your customer is $135.

What if they spend an average of $25 every month going forward (after month 4)?

That means from month 5-12 they will spend $200.00 (and however long going forward).

So, let me ask the question again...

What if I said it cost you $135 to obtain the same customer? Is it worth it?

You bet!

Sure, you are 'break even' for the first four months, but after that — new customer, new income.

Once the cycle is up and running you are in great shape. Those new customers you found five months ago are now paying for the obtaining of new customers today! And you can build it bigger and bigger.

DISCLAIMER ONE: Now, this is an incredibly simplistic example that has some additional variables on either side. Profitability of cookies (cost of goods) on one side vs the multitude of ways we could get the cost of acquisition down just by tweaking some things in our campaign... but you get the idea.

DISCLAIMER TWO: I like oatmeal raisin cookies if you are looking to send me cookies.

An ONLINE business is no different.

If you are trying to sell a product or service online, the process is still the same.

- ✓ What is the cost to obtain a lead?
- ✓ What is the cost to obtain a customer?
- ✓ What is the lifetime value of a customer?

Even at the very basic short-term relationship you can come up with a value.

Let's say you are selling a *How to Care for Your Pet Mouse* online training.

You charge people $19.95 to take the training.

If you paid the same as our brick and mortar example earlier, it doesn't work.

100 people equals 5 sales ($20 per acquisition).

Since you charge $19.95 for your training, you lost $.05

You need to either raise the price of your training (and hope you get the same number of buyers) or better define the ad.

This is where drilling down on your audience will really help turn an ok campaign into a killer campaign!

Maybe after looking at the data you find out *only women are taking the class* and cut your advertisement to only display to women.

Now maybe for every 100 women that see the ad, 12 sign up.

Now your cost is $8.33 per acquisition (100/12).

Ta Da - You made money!

So, even if you only have ONE product to sell, and a very short "lifetime value," there is still SOME value and ways to determine how much you need to make back on a sale.

Now come out with a sequel to *How to Care for Your Pet Mouse*.

You know something like, "How to help your Cat not be jealous of your Pet Mouse"

Boom, something else to sell and add to the lifetime value of a customer!

Action Items.

You know, the kind of thing Limes work on:

- Check out what ads your competition might be running on Facebook.

- Check out BeTheLime.com for more Facebook advertising tips.

BE THE LIME

Chapter Seven:

SOMETIMES IT IS JUST SIMPLE ENHANCEMENT OR DUPLICATION.

"In school, my favorite subject was math. That's where I learned to count money."

- French Montana

When it comes to bringing your business or your brand to the next level, you have two proven strategies right out of the gate.

Enhancement or Duplication.

With *Enhancement,* you are going to *add* something to your existing product that has greater perceived value. You are going to improve it.

For example, if you are selling bottled water from an ancient spring but NOW you add Vitamin C to the water...boom...you have an addition.

Spring Water Now Enriched with Vitamin C.

You have added something (feature or benefit) to an existing product.

It is certainly helpful when the *Enhancement* is something people are looking for, but often it does not need to be.

I could say, **"Be The Lime Spring Water Now With Spring Fed Castershock™!"**

People would be looking down at their own, now inferior, bottled water, without **Castershock™**. They will wonder why their bottle of water does not have it. What are they missing out on? How much better is water with **Castershock™**?

Of course, "**Castershock™**" is just a made up word (or at least I hope it is).

Side Note: Throw in a trademark symbol and that MUST be some serious stuff. Perception becomes reality.

Enhancement is usually about "improving" an existing product in the eyes of the consumer.

- ✓ Now with 20% More Peanuts!
- ✓ New and Improved.
- ✓ Now with Stain Fighter Action
- ✓ 100% Gluten Free
- ✓ Still a Pint!

The last one is from a Ben and Jerry's ice cream campaign.

When the industry started making their ice cream containers slightly smaller, they still calling them a 'pint'. Yep…they were ripping us off.

Ben and Jerry's actually pulled off an *Enhancement* without actually doing anything.

There was no real 'improvement' – <u>staying the same</u> became the ***Enhancement***.

You have to appreciate the genius in that!

Sometimes you can make improvements to your product or brand, sometimes you can't.

Usually improvements come from features that customers are requesting or what you see competitors doing.

The other option is **Duplication** and oftentimes, this can lead to a large jump in your business.

As opposed to improving or enhancing an existing product, you are going to offer **more** products. Additional products that are similar in nature, *but now you are offering choices.*

Coca-Cola was around 100 years before they ever felt the need, or pressure, to clone the model across new brands.

Nearly 98 years after successfully creating and marketing the original, Coca-Cola, they added Diet Coke.

When I last looked online, Coca-Cola had somewhere around 25 different core brands...and then subsets of each of those brands.

All said, there must be a couple hundred varieties of brands they control!

Don't believe me? Just search the Google for brands owned by Coca-Cola. You will be amazed...brands you have never even heard of!

Coca-Cola used **Duplication** in a market that began to require it. If you didn't expand, you got left behind.

Too much shelf space was being eaten up by new and upstart brands. And in the soda world, shelf space is key.

So...

Coca-Cola knocks out a few new types of beverages and different flavors within them. Cherry Coke, Coke with Lime*, etc.

*I like to think the Lime was added for me...but probably not.

Coca-Cola used **Duplication** successfully.

Apple has done the same thing with the iPhone.

Take a look at the release list below...

- 1st gen: June 29, 2007
- 3G: July 11, 2008
- 3GS: June 19, 2009
- 4: June 24, 2010
- 4S: October 14, 2011
- 5: September 21, 2012
- 5C, 5S: September 20, 2013
- 6/6 Plus: September 19, 2014
- 6S/6S Plus: September 25, 2015
- SE: March 31, 2016
- 7/7 Plus: September 16, 2016

From 2007 to 2012 the iPhone enjoyed an "**Enhancement**" strategy. The model 'improved' each year.

In 2013 Apple began to offer additional choices. In addition to the new "best iPhone ever," there was a **Duplication**: The 5C was introduced.

In 2014 Apple had another multiplication, offering the relatively same model, but in two different sizes (6 and 6 Plus).

Apple is currently operating both *Enhancement* and *Duplication* strategies in its iPhone line...and cashing in during the process.

Frankly, everyone who geeks out on marketing, including myself, is guilty of using Apple, Coca-Cola, BMW, Sony, etc. as examples. Too much in fact.

The small or medium size business or brand feels detached thinking these things are just for the "big boys." Advanced strategies for those with big budgets or staff.

Nothing could be further from the truth...

This is not just a 'big company' strategy. Almost any company can benefit from *Enhancement* or *Duplication*.

The person with the small cupcake shop can add a larger variety of cupcakes and offer a larger selection.

The person with a hair cutting salon can add a nail booth and a chair massage station. This 'one-stop-shop' gains business (and revenue) because of it.

Gas stations now offer gas, soda, and even made-to-order sandwiches and frozen yogurt.

Enhancement and *Duplication.*

Sometimes you can offer *both*.

A restaurant offering 'more choices' and 'better ingredients.'

And this is <u>not</u> limited to hard goods at a brick and mortar store.

Maybe you teach or sell something online.

How to bake cookies, play guitar, invest in cars, weave baskets, or build a rocket ship.

Can you offer more classes? Maybe add an "advanced" class?

Adding more types or levels of trainings would be a *Duplication*. What if you also delivered those classes via a couple different methods, such as video, printed transcript, and audio files.

Now you have an *Enhancement* and a *Duplication*.

Action Items.

You know, the kind of thing Limes work on:

- Take a look your own business or brand.

- Do you largely market your business or brand based on *Enhancement* or *Duplication*? If you have only done one method, how could you implement the other?

Chapter Eight:

DO THEY NEED, WANT, OR LIKE YOU?

"I'm not bad. I'm just drawn that way."

– Jessica Rabbit

Let's get needy for a minute.

Do your customers NEED you, WANT you, or do they LIKE you?

There is a very important difference between these three when it comes to marketing yourself or your product.

You need to know this in order to properly communicate with your people.

Really, sometimes it is as different as Apples & Oranges.

Let's get away from Limes for a second and let's say I have an online apple website *(or an apple brick and mortar business)*. I am known as the apple expert. I sell...

✓ Red Delicious
✓ Honeycrisp
✓ Cripps Pink
✓ Golden Delicious
✓ Braeburn
✓ Gravenstien
✓ Jonagold
✓ Gala and
✓ Winesap
✓ *And many other types of apples.*

Those are all real apples by the way...I looked it up!

But let's say every time you get an email from me, I am sending you stuff about oranges.

Every "special" you see on the board when you come into my store is about oranges.

I even started wearing orange shirts.

Would you say there is a disconnect?

You bet.

You would be confused and I would certainly lose your business. You were in a "relationship" with me for the apples. Not oranges, not grapefruits, not dates.

If I am the apple expert, I am going to send you recipes on pies, drinks, dried apples, apple cider, and clothes made out of apples.*

I don't think you can make clothes out of apples, but someone reading this will prove me wrong.

I need to focus on what brought us together and make sure that ANY interaction we have reinforces that fact.

My marketing message should start with that.

Let's try something shall we?

I want you to make a list of three things that come to mind. They need to be places you shop or companies you purchase from, something where there is some sort of interaction.

Here is my off-the-top-of-head-list.

1. GolfNow
2. Netflix
3. Dropbox

Now, let's take them one by one.

GolfNow

GolfNow is an app on my phone (they also have a desktop version) where you can go online and get substantially discounted rounds of golf.

I am often wanting to go out golfing "last minute." You know, waking up in the morning and wondering if there is a tee time in an hour or so that I can get out and play.

GolfNow fits that want.

I don't **NEED** GolfNow. There are other Apps out there. I do **LIKE** GolfNow, it serves and performs its purpose.

Most of GolfNow's communications are straight to the point. "Grab this tee time for 50% off."

Knowing that they have competitors, GolfNow, in addition to maintaining their relationships with golf courses, needs to focus on two things.

Maintain a no hassle use for people like me looking to get out and golf and...

...make sure I know they are the best.

Their communications with me need to reinforce convenience and best pricing.

I want to golf and don't want to call around to a bunch of courses looking for a tee time.

RESULT: I both LIKE and NEED GolfNow

Netflix

Ok, I clearly don't NEED Netflix*

*unless we are talking the series **Stranger Things.**

I LIKE Netflix.

At about $10 per month, it is a whole lot of entertainment for those nights that I am looking for some sort of distraction.

Although there are actually plenty of competitors out there for Netflix, their communications to me need to focus on why I am with Netflix in the first place.

Netflix is a monthly fee, so they need to be sure there is no drama in our relationship other than their shows.

I WANT to see the shows that are on Netflix.

It is the same reason both Netflix and HBO have begun creating their own programs – they need an edge from each other.

Like **Game of Thrones**? Well, you are going to need an HBO subscription. Like **House of Cards**? Well, come on over to Netflix.

Things like this are just burning the networks left and right. What? Commercial free programming AND original works?!

I would love to be in THAT boardroom discussion.

Result: I both LIKE and WANT Netflix

Dropbox

Dropbox is a program that allows me to easily store and shares files online.

With technology the way it is, there are often challenges when we try to share info.

For example, if I need to send my publisher a picture, in high resolution, chances are the file is too big to send via email.

Sure, I could burn it to a disk or a USB drive, but now I have to mail it to him—and time is of the essence*.

Either due to reality or my general impatience nowadays...not sure which.

Enter Dropbox.

I upload the file, send a link to whomever and *voila*, they have the file.

As a matter of fact, you've probably already experienced this (if only behind the scenes) when you get free special reports from BeTheLime.com

Result: Trifecta. I NEED, WANT, and LIKE Dropbox.

At the end of the day, the ONLY way you are going to get business is if they Want, Like, or Need you.

Needing is of course the best.

These are things you can't live without.

If I need a certain medication, I am not going to skip it and sever that relationship. Heck, I don't even have to like you if you are the only one that can supply me with the needed medication.

Wanting is very strong.

Someone wanting your brand, but can quickly go away if something better comes along. How can you keep them wanting you?

Like is pretty weak.

Continuing to support your business or brand based just on like does not go very far.

We all like the local hardware store that can fit in the average size home. It comes with some 100-year-old guy that knows everything. We really LIKE that guy. But, Home Depot is down the street and the local hardware store is going the way of the dinosaur.

Figure out what your brand is and deal with it accordingly. Can you elevate it? I bet you can!

Action Items.

You know, the kind of thing Limes work on:

- Make a list of three things and decide whether they are a Need, Want, or Like for you.

- Think about HOW they communicate with you, if at all. How should they be communicating with you?

- Now, make a list of people that are paying attention to your product or brand. How should you communicate with them based on whether they Want, Like, or Need you?

Chapter Ten:

BUILDING A SOLID LIST OF CUSTOMERS

"My New Year's Resolution List usually starts with the desire to lose between ten and three thousand pounds."

- Nia Vardalos

What is a list of customers?

A "list" is basically a collection of information you have on your clients or customers.

At the most basic level, it is having their email address. **EVERY LIME** should have an email list of clients, customers, and prospects.

Since we do most of Be The Lime marketing *online*, I am most concerned with getting an email address.

Having an email address on file means we can market to them whenever we want, at essentially zero cost.

Proper list building and marketing can add a substantial boost to the bottom line of almost any business (even if you think yours does not apply...guess again).

First, let's start with a fun, real world, example.

Let's say you own a small restaurant that specializes in seafood. For the weekend, you order 50 pounds of Halibut to be delivered on Thursday.

When the order comes in you accidently get 500 pounds of Halibut (which frankly sounds like a lot of Halibut).

After a lengthy conversation with your Halibut supplier, you both agree that the additional 450 pounds is yours at an amazing discount unheard of in the Halibut industry (or whatever one would call it).

Things are about to get fishy!

No time for any traditional print media promotion.

You can throw a sign out front, but what are the odds that someone walks by with a Halibut craving?

Hopefully, you do have one ace in the hole!

You have an email list of people that come in to your restaurant and you have permission to contact them.

Well, it is time to call in that mark.

You walk over to your computer and type out a short email. If I were writing the email for you, it might look something like this...

Email Subject Line: *How I gained 450 pounds...of Halibut.*

Our fresh fish company just made a whale of a mistake...

...actually a halibut of a mistake.

They just sent me an extra 450 pounds of premium Halibut filets. I am talking top shelf stuff!

When I tried to send them back, they offered me an amazing price I could not refuse.

I mean this is once-in-a-lifetime kind of pricing

and I am passing it on to you.

Here is the deal...

Come in Friday or Saturday night for Buy One, Get One on Halibut filets!

Our only rule is when they are gone, they are gone.

Hard to believe, but at this price, I will go through all 450 pounds...FAST!

Yep...we are getting our Halibut on. The Distributer's loss is our gain!

Call 555-555-5555 to reserve your table now!

See you this weekend,

Frank
Frank's Seafood Stop

P.S. This really is a once-in-a-lifetime deal and I am sharing this with my best customers. Make your reservation now (555-555-5555)

Now send the email out to your list. Cost to market: Pretty much ZERO!

If you have been building your list and courting them correctly, you will not only get some great email responses, you will get a big hit on reservations for the weekend and unload that Halibut*

*Here is one interesting fact. Many of the people that come in may not even order the Halibut. But your email reminded them of you, your restaurant, and how they would love to come by again. Either way, you made money off your list.

I know what you are saying.

"Fred, I don't own a restaurant. I just sell xyz or service xyz clients."

Well, I don't care if you sell rocks or provide a service that cleans rocks. There is a list to be built and money to be made from it!

I have had clients with all sorts of products. *Many of which I had no idea that existed.*

Even some of the more bizarre ones still had other people with the same interests that were out there looking for information. When that happens...ta da....a list is born.

There are lots of ways to communicate with your "list." I think email is one of the best ways to get an immediate response from your list.

Having a list of people you can market to can be an invaluable profit center when you need it most. Your list might contain:

Raving fans
Potential clients
Colleagues
New prospects

Previous buyers
Preferred buyers

You may have heard, when it comes to marketing your business online, that the "money is in the list."

Although that is true to some extent, the fact of the matter is that the money is in your RELATIONSHIP with the list.

Let's go over a few List Building basics and see how it might fit into your business.

How do I start a list?

There are many ways to get a list going. Personally I like online the best. There are some great companies out there that make list building online an easy to manage process (go to Be TheLime.com/EmailServices to see our favorites).

Let's just say that people who visit your website have the opportunity to sign up and get on your list. I am sure you have seen this many times on sites you have visited.

Rule #1 – Why should I sign up for your emails?

This is a big question you better be able to answer.

When people come to your site and are presented with an email sign up, they know what is coming: emails.

People get plenty of emails, so they want to know if they sign up for one more message there will be something more valuable than cluttering their inbox. This is done in two ways:

A Bribe or Ongoing Info (preferably both).

A bribe is something the person will immediately get:free lunch, an extra piece of pie, 50% off their next purchase, special report on unicorns.

It is called a "bribe" because that is just what you are doing.

You are bribing them for an email address, in exchange, you will give them a shiny object they want.

It is not a bad thing.

It is a just a fair exchange of information. Their email in exchange for [insert bribe here].

I am presented with these all the time online. Sometimes I find the bribe worth it and sign up...other times I don't.

Most people are of an "immediate" benefit mentality. So an *immediate bribe* is usually the best route.

The other route is an "Ongoing" benefit.

You have to be careful with this.

You don't want to give people the impression that they will see their inbox jammed with emails from you every hour.

I would say something like; "From time to time we pass on special opportunities to our exclusive guests via email."

Sounds fairly safe to me but also a weaker incentive – *no immediate benefit.*

Rule #2 – See Double

No matter what type of "bribe" you offer, with few exceptions, I recommend using what is called "Double Opt-in."

This is an industry standard that protects those signing up on your list (and ensures you have valid emails).

Basically, the user must "confirm" their sign up by clicking a link sent to the email address they signed up with.

It also means that you are not spamming anyone.

Your list provider is more likely to be happy with you when a few complaints come in – "Hey; THEY signed up for it (and "Double Opt-in" is your proof)."

Rule #3 – Be Professional

Don't be a Lemon

I want to mention three things here...

- ✓ Don't send out emails too often.

- ✓ Don't send emails that have nothing to do with why they signed up for in the first place.

✓ Don't make every email about selling them something.

I will cover these three items in greater detail in the "Email" chapter, but thought I better mention it here before someone runs off and builds (and burns) a list before getting to that chapter.

By the way, "professional" does not mean you can't have fun or be personable with your list. Quite the opposite, in fact.

But I Don't Have a Restaurant!

Still "hooked" on that restaurant example aren't you? Ok...

The fact of the matter is just about anyone can build a list of raving and responsive fans. Don't think for a second you even have to have a brick and mortar store.

Many people have businesses that exist ONLY online.

For those businesses, online list building can be the biggest factor in success or failure.

As a matter of fact, if you show me a successful online business that is not building and utilizing a list, I will show you a company that could probably double or even triple their profits!

What about people that walk into my business (ie: not on the website)?

There are many ways to handle people that are "in person" but the rules are very much the same.

They need a reason to give you an email.

Remember the old "Drop your business card to win a free lunch?" Yep, that was a bribe!

In person, they still need to have a reason, but also a BIGGER reason if you want to get them on the Double Opt-in list.

It may be worth the expense of having an Apple iPad or similar device; right up front were people can sign up online.

You might be surprised if you ask people in person, and have the right bribe, you will get a lot of sign ups.

List Building and Beyond

List building goes well beyond the scope of promoting just your own stuff. A well-managed list can yield additional income and opportunities on so many levels.

You may not have anything to "sell" your list. Even if that is the case (which I am finding hard to believe) you are going to want to stay in contact with them with periodic updates.

In the end, whatever your business, List Building needs to be a part of it (minus the Halibut).

Action Items.

You know, the kind of thing Limes work on:

- Check out the online list building tools at BeTheLime.com

- Create a "Bribe" for your audience

- Make a list of "Non Sales" topics you can share with your list over time. They MUST be interesting and have real value.

- Read the "Email Marketing" chapter for tips and tricks on what do say in your emails.

Fred's note: No Halibuts were harmed in this chapter. The Halibuts mentioned are works of fiction. Any actual Halibuts in real life resembling those mentioned in this chapter are purely coincidental.

BE THE LIME

Chapter Eleven:

WEBSITES -
THE FINAL ANSWER

"Everything You Read On the
Internet is Probably True."

- Abraham Lincoln

I can't believe I still have to have the conversation about whether or not someone's business should have a website?

Why don't we start the conversation on whether or not you need to have a phone? Or air to breathe?

No matter what the size of your business or brand, big or small, you have a problem.

As a matter of fact, it doesn't matter who you are. Man or woman, wealthy or just scraping by; we ALL have the same problem.

Lack of Time.

How you invest that time is important. Chances are, no one knows that more than you.

Today's business owner often feels that they are getting pulled in a million different directions, and for the most part, they are.

The advancements in technology were supposed to give us more time. In a lot of cases, it has given us less.

Those of us who are old enough to remember a time before computers can barely remember what we did without them, but we seemed to get along just fine.

Look! Shiny object!

Now there are too many things trying to get our attention, and they do so with utmost efficiency.

So much so, that some companies even block sites like Facebook so their employees are not losing countless hours checking in with friends when they should be working.

Of course, this no longer works as the employee has a secret weapon.

Enter the "smartphone."

Controlling the office computer network is circumvented by the employee simply pulling out their smartphone to check Twitter, Facebook, etc., all from the palm of their hand.

People are distracted by emails & social media and they don't even have to be at a computer.

Just walk into any restaurant and take a look at the people dining. A large number will be checking in on their phones numerous times during the meal, if not glued to it the entire time.

This IS the market we have today. This is the market we MUST deal with.

Your marketing message must cut through the noise.

Your customer (or potential customer) is going through the exact same thing as everyone else. They are overwhelmed.

Your marketing messages are not only competing against your competitors, they are competing against Angry Birds™, Words with Friends™, and countless kitten videos.

Somehow you need to get your message through all that noise and make a connection!

Some companies spend millions of dollars trying to get the consumers attention. They buy million-dollar television ads only to have the consumer "fast forward" through the commercials on their DVR.

Offline marketing is nearly dead.

Newspapers and magazines are closing their doors left and right. The ones that are surviving have turned to online solutions for a lifeboat.

The fact of the matter is, like it or not, in today's marketing people are glued to their phones, tablets, and computers.

You can buy the largest billboard on the largest corner of the largest park in your town. Chances are, most of the people walking by were looking down at their phones and never saw your message.

The natural evolution, in all business marketing, was to turn to the Internet.

First rule of marketing: You go where the people are.

You need to be "in the game" to have a chance.

Enter: Websites

The Internet, and specifically Websites, has afforded four incredible gifts to the entrepreneur. Websites are...

- ✓ Affordable

- ✓ Easy to Leverage

- ✓ Fast to Market

- ✓ A Great Equalizer

Let me explain these in opposite order starting with my favorite.

A Great Equalizer

I love this part.

You may have 500 employees making stuffed unicorns in a factory and sell your product online.

You can have a picture of your building, your staff, a warehouse, a shipping truck, a mail center, and of course your product.

At the end of the day, you are competing directly with the stay-at-home mom that has created a four-page website promoting unicorns and offering the plush toy for sale via an online shopping cart.

The stay-at-home-mom wins.

In today's world, the stay-at-home mom can actually beat the big company in search rankings, traffic, and even sales.

The potential customer does not really care what is "behind" the website. They are looking for a connection. They are looking, in this case, to buy a stuffed unicorn and may the best man (or woman) win.

The stay-at-home-mom (okay, or dad) can react fast when it comes to the latest trend or current marketing story. If "unicorn" news comes up, he/she can have a story on his/her website within minutes while the big corporation needs to run it by every mid-level manager to get "approval."

On the Internet, big marketing teams give way to the personal opinions of a well-spoken individual.

Having a "voice" is key, and often times the big corporations don't have one.

Speed to Market

My company (Exposure One) can build a website in a day. In a couple hours if the content is ready to go.

Within hours of going "live" I can send traffic to the site using a variety of methods discussed in this book.

If there is a breaking news topic out there, and I have an established website, I might write a post and be on the #1 of Google in a matter of minutes.

There are no committees; there are no significant approval processes. There is just speed.

Need to make a change to an article? Within 30

seconds the rest of the online world has an updated article in front of them. Want to post an entirely new article, photo, or video? Time is measured in minutes, not hours or days.

This speed is important to small business owners for one very big reason.

Large companies cannot move fast. They have an approval process. They have several departments that have to sign-off before something can be published or modified.

You have no such worries or trappings. You are lean. You can turn your ship on a dime and beat the other guys to the deal.

Even if you are not competing against a big corporation, you are competing against someone (or something).

Speed to market is your ace in the hole when it comes to being current.

Leverage

Remember in the introduction when we spoke about "time?"

You don't have the time to be on the Internet all day. Heck, you probably don't want to.

Find a single action that can be replicated without more effort (or time) and can yield bigger results.

If you were to speak to a prospective customer, one-on-one at a local diner, you might make a deal at the end of the day. Then again, it might be a huge waste of time.

That same speech can be given at a local Chamber of Commerce meeting in front of dozens of people, netting you multiple new customers on one effort.

Take that same speech, create a video, and put it on the web, and you are in a whole different ball game when it comes to leverage.

You are no longer bound by the size of a building, seating, or even a geographic location. Furthermore, you don't need to pick a time of day.

If someone wants to hear your message at 9:00 am, they can. If someone else wants to read your article at 3:12 am in Hawaii, they can as well.

Websites are the ultimate workhorse; 24 hours a day, seven days a week!

Out to Lunch (but still working).

You would be amazed at the number of people who check out your website in the middle of the night.

If you run a business, you probably were not in your office at 11:30 pm taking calls.

Guess what?

People are online all hours of the day and your website is ready for them.

With so many items sucking the time out of you, websites give you a leg up when it comes to marketing.

Affordable

The days of websites being a financial barrier are gone. Don't let anyone tell you differently.

When we created Exposure One, the first thing new clients were amazed with (and still are to this day) is that our prices seemed crazy low.

Well, they are low.

That is not because we could not charge more. We should. The fact of the matter is that most companies are out there are convincing people websites are still so hard to build.

That is just not true.

Sure, you can have a very difficult site to build. One with more bells and whistles than anything ever seen...and for that, you can spend big bucks. But those are getting rare.

The average small business or brand site built by our company costs between $500 - $800.

Price is no longer a barrier to a quality, easy-to-use website. Heck, you can even build one yourself!

So, what changed this world and made sites affordable to the average consumer?

WordPress and Themes

Wordpress is a foundation that allows users to interact with their site (add new posts, make content changes, post photos, etc) with ease.

It exists "behind the scenes" on a website. But, and this is the important part, it made it easy for the casual user to update, change, and modify the site.

If you have been on the Internet, you have been on a Wordpress site...you just didn't know it because they look like every other site.

In fact, the last numbers I heard was that nearly 20% of all sites on the Internet were run on Wordpress.

You have a business to promote. Want to spend time making changes and additions to your website instead of learning complex programming? WordPress gives you that power.

You no longer need to call your programmer and pay him or her $50 for a change to your website. Chances are, you can do it yourself, in minutes, with ease.

Of course the existence of WordPress alone was not enough. That is where "Themes" come in.

Themes (or "templates") are what the site looks like. It's what people see when they go to your site.

Themes can look like whatever you want them to. Colors, graphics, layouts, etc.

There are thousands of themes to choose from.

You can modify themes with relative ease or get one custom made. Trust me, whatever you want your site to look like, someone has a theme that is pretty damn close, if not right on target.

The cost of a theme? Anywhere from $0.00 to $200.

For the most part you will probably spend $50 on a nice looking theme that fits your needs. To learn more about themes, you can read a post about them at BetheLime.com.

Yep, gone are the days when the big guys ruled the web due to the cost barrier of website creation. Wordpress and Themes were a game changer.

Small is the new Big - A small business owner's biggest mistake.

There is a big trend going on online right now and it will dramatically change local businesses and how they are served up online.

Is the web too big now for small business?

Many small business owners think the web is too big.

It is world-wide after all and some owners think since their business or brand is in a small or medium size town that they will get little or no benefit from a website.

False. Nothing could be further from the truth.

Everyone benefits by an online presence.

Frankly, at this moment, I suspect I am preaching to the choir or you wouldn't be reading this book. But it is worth making sure we are all on the same page.

Internet search engines have a problem.

There is too much stuff out there.

More and more people are searching for what they need...and they need it NOW.

If someone living in Wells, NV searches for "Birthday Cakes" and gets search results in California, New York, and London, the search was a bust.

They want to buy a cake, not go on a trip.

Google™ and many of the other search engines are changing (almost daily) how and what results come up when you search.

They may not show you the biggest company site, the most visited, or even the most talked about.

Nope, they are serving up what they believe is the most RELEVANT to what you might be looking for.

This is both a big change and a big opportunity for the little guy!

Many "early adopter" businesses that have concentrated on their websites have taken their local competition by surprise.

They saw it coming.

If that was you, great. If not, don't worry. There is still plenty of time to put your stake in the ground and capture some market.

What is all this about 'mobile' traffic?

For the purpose of this chapter I wanted to turn your attention to websites.

But you should be aware of a very important "split" going on right now.

It is between websites that are being viewed on a computer and websites that are being viewed on a phone.

Although they are both looking for something, there could be, depending on what they searching for, a different urgency in what comes up in the rankings.

If, in the course of this book I talk about the Internet, I am always talking about both groups.

To not leave you hanging on this "mobile" discussion I will leave you with this:

Your site, at the very least, will need to be "mobile optimized." That means that it looks good on a mobile phone. The user does not have to pinch in and out to read it.

The bottom line…. Can people find you?

Your customers, clients, and perspective businesses are online. They are on the web.

Sure, you may have the rare business that offline marketing is the way to go but I would bet your business would be even bigger if you focused some attention to online marketing (and that does not mean paying for ads).

People are using the Internet more and more to solve an immediate need. Your business or product needs to be easily found.

Websites are affordable, fast, leverage your marketing efforts, and are the great equalizer.

If you already have a website, then we just need to make sure you are using it to its fullest potential (Pro Tip: Most companies are not even close).

Dollar for dollar, there is not a better place for you to have a presence in today's marketing than a website.

Action Items.

You know, the kind of thing Limes work on:

- If you don't have a website, now is the time to start.

- If you do have a website, is it mobile optimized?

- What is the goal of your website? Promoting your brand or getting people to take some sort of action?

BE THE LIME

Chapter Twelve:

SHOULD YOU PAY TO ADVERTISE?

"Advertising is only evil when it advertises evil things."

– David Ogivly

How many times have you been watching a television show and wished, "Man, I wish they would show more commercials!"

I am going to guess somewhere around zero.*

Ok, I will give you commercials during the Super Bowl. Those can be entertaining. But those are the ONLY ones, unless you are really weird, or an advertising executive.

I can't say that the online environment is much different. People are not really looking for ads. Which means the smart advertisers are getting better and better at vying for the user's attention. You want to be a smart advertiser.

So, why advertise online?

The fact of the matter is that advertising can get your message out to a whole lot of people in a real hurry.

Take Google™ for instance.

If you type in just about any search term, you will be given a list of sites. The top two or three are going to be paid ads. People bid for those spots.

There is no guarantee they have a good product or bad product...just that they were willing to pay the most money if someone clicked on their ad.

But...in a matter of hours, you could be at the top of a search result!

Learn the Lingo...

When you buy ads, there are typically three terms you will hear often.

Cost Per Click (CPC) and Pay Per Click (PPC)

Cost Per Thousand Views (CPM)

Basically, they are two DIFFERENT ways to advertise (and pay).

For example...

You might pay $3.00 on a PPC campaign. That means you ONLY pay when someone clicks on your actual ad. It doesn't matter how many people SEE the ad, just how many click on it.

Every time someone clicks on your ad, you pay $3.00. You control your spending with a max daily budget.

The terms CPC and PPC are often used as the same, but in reality, they are slightly different.

You might "bid" $3.00 for a click (PPC) but actually pay something less at the end of the day (CPC).

I like to think of CPC as being my "actual end of the day cost" of a click. The more efficient my campaign becomes, the less my out of pocket cost (CPC) may be.

With CPM, you are paying for people to SEE the ad. It does not matter how many people click on the ad

– but the cost (per impression) is cheap. Let's say $.04 per 1,000 views.

So, which is better? CPC or CPM?

For the most part, CPC will be better. You will only pay when you have a lead. With CPM you are paying whether people click or not.

Occasionally, if you have a really hot performing ad, CPM might net you a lower advertising cost...so it is always worth testing if you find that you are getting a lot of clicks.

CPM may also work when you are targeting very small groups (under 1500).

Where to start

The big three places to start advertising are...

- ✓ Facebook

- ✓ Yahoo

- ✓ Google

All three are very easy to use and have a lot of options to help you target your audience.

Depending on your business, you are probably going to want to focus locally, so you will want to pay attention to "where" your ad is running. It doesn't do any good to have a local restaurant in Miami, FL and be paying for an ad in Wells, NV.

I am pretty sure, no matter how good the ad is, they are not getting in the car and driving to see you and yet you just paid for the click.

Other options to choose from might include age, education level, income, and a host of other choices.

The more you know your audience *(remember that Avatar Chapter?)*, the more you can target your ads and save money in the process.

Manage your budget.

When starting out, you are going to want to test a couple different ads. Different headlines, copy, and pictures.

You might be surprised to hear that a small change to an ad can make a big difference in its performance.

Additionally, make sure you set limits on the spending. Any reputable advertising service empowers you to choose a daily budget.

If you set your daily budget at $20 per day...once you have spent $20 in clicks, the ad will stop running for the remainder of the day. It will then "reset" at midnight.

Oftentimes you can set a "campaign" limit as well.

You determine a flat dollar amount. Once that amount has been spent in ads, the campaign stops running. This gives you a chance to evaluate the data and see if you want to tweak the ad or restart.

But Fred, What about "FREE" Ads?

Some sites such as Craigslist can be a great source for free advertising.

Although you are not paying for the ads, the same rules of engagement apply. Test multiple ads.

With free ads, you will need to separate yourself from the pack. There will be more ads in the free environment, so you need to stand out.

The good news is that most of the free ads I have seen on Craigslist and other sites, are not that hard to beat. They are usually put together with poor grammar or no real compelling information to take action. Just adding some pictures is a big plus.

Spend some time going through ads (paid and free) and see which ones you think are good.

Don't copy them word for word, but you can use them for "research" and create your own ad.

Some people pay copywriters big bucks…no reason not to piggyback their efforts.

Tips for Writing Ads

You basically only need three things for a good ad. But, you can spend a lot of time on each of them:

- ✓ Intriguing Headline

- ✓ A Clear Selling Proposition

✓ Good Call To Action

Think of your ad as a billboard. The Headline needs to grab the reader's attention.

The copy should be intriguing. There needs to be a proposition that makes people want to find out more.

There needs to be a call to action! "Click here for my Free Report." Or "Check out our Free Information Now!"

Keep it Fresh!

On Facebook, thirty-seven percent of respondents refresh their ad creative once every 5-14 days, while another 20 percent only change it up as often as every 15-29 days. [Source SocialFresh.com]

As I mentioned earlier, you are going to want to test more than one version of an ad (to find the top performer).

But even when you have a top performer, it will only last so long before readers start to ignore it. So be prepared to have a new version ready to step in!

Make sure your photo (if available in your ad) makes sense.

They say a "Picture is worth a thousand words." That is helpful when you can have a photo in your ad, but not so much if the photo turns people off or doesn't make sense.

WHO do you advertise to?

As I have mentioned, there are plenty of demographics at your disposal when it comes to placing ads.

Knowing your customer could never be more important than at this time.

Maybe most of your customers that come in the store are men. But maybe the customers who spend more when they are in the store are women.

For all the downside of personal privacy being thrown by the wayside, it is an advertiser's dream.

If you want to target 24-35 year-old, non-married women, who like cats, the Dave Matthews Band, and live in Texas, believe it or not, you can probably target your ads to ONLY show up to that group.

"Custom Lists" can be gold...

This is one of my favorite ways to advertise, especially in the beginning if you can tap into a list.

Let's say that you build websites for Real Estate Agents in your town and surrounding cities and you would like to run a Facebook ad.

Without much effort you could obtain a list of Real Estate Agents in your area. You could buy a list of names, search for them online, and look in the yellow pages.

In Facebook Advertising, you can create a "custom list."

Now, you UPLOAD those names into a list you name something like "RE45." I don't like to make the list name too obvious, but I still know what it is.

Facebook will now search all those email you uploaded to see who has a matching Facebook account (created with that email).

Now you can create an advertisement that ONLY is displayed to people on your "RE45" list.

Wow, talk about targeted!

Now, certainly not all of them are going to match up.

Some people will have used a different email address to sign up for Facebook. But even if 50% of them do, you are well on your way!

But it doesn't stop there! You can use that list to have Facebook create you a similar list.

Facebook will look for what all those people have in common and try to find similarities.

Now, that might not work for targeting Real Estate agents (since we already know who they are) but imagine the possibilities in generating new clients in other areas.

Before you go wild creating custom lists and go on an ad-buying spree, you must…

Measure Your Results

One thing people often forget is to <u>measure the results</u>.

Let's say you place an ad and pay a total of $100 during its run.

And let's say that during that run, 200 people clicked over to your site.

That means you paid $.50 per lead.

Sounds good, but was it successful?

Well, what were they supposed to do AFTER they clicked on your ad? Buy something? Come into your store?

Traffic, for the sake of traffic, is not necessarily a winning campaign. You need to attach something you can measure.

For example...

Let's say that IF someone clicks on your ad they are presented a coupon. IF they bring that coupon into your business they get a free cookie.

You know that 200 people clicked on the ad. If 10 people came in with the coupon and claimed their cookie, your true lead cost is $10 per lead. ($100 divided by 10).

As you continue to test, you may discover that 150 of 200 people clicking were men, but only 1 of the 10 people that showed up at the store were men (9 were women).

So, clearly when it comes to actually coming into the store and spending money, women were converting better.

Now you would go back to you campaign and target "women only" with the ad.

In keeping with our example...50 clicks would cost $25. Nine women come into the store so now your lead cost was only $2.78. *Now you are getting the idea!*

Test it out for yourself

The bottom line is that placing ads is certainly worth testing. You may find it to be a great source of leads and business!

I had a client the other day who was discussing two different ads to run on Facebook.

He was wrestling with which one to run (they both fed the same campaign/product sale).

He spent about 15 minutes going back and forth of the benefits of one over the other.

He, finally, asked me what I thought.

I said, "Jim, I am going to give you a great cop out answer...and it took me years and years and years of experience to get to share this knowledge with you. Try both."

The fact of the matter is that we can only put our best foot forward. Testing is key.

Sure, I can create a couple of ads based on years of experience and brand awareness, but at the end of the day, I am not the buyer, and sometimes you just never know what they will react to.

Testing a couple different ads is easy. But you MUST know the outcome of each ad, all the way down to the buy, sign up, or whatever the desired action is.

Action Items.

You know, the kind of thing Limes work on:

- Run a search in Google for your type of business. What Ads pop up? What happens if you click on the ads? What does the competition do with the lead?

- Check out Facebook. Are there any "groups" or pages that have similar interests as your business?

- Create an ad using three parts. Headline, Selling Proposition, Call to Action.

Chapter Thirteen:

MARKETING TO YOUR EMAIL LIST.

*"Permission Marketing is the tool
that unlocks the power of the Internet."*

– Seth Godin

In a previous chapter, I discussed the benefits of having a customer list: Email being the most cost effective around.

In this chapter I want to talk about what to *do* with that list of emails. As a matter of fact, in just a minute, I am going to give you actual strategies you can use today!

In 1992, the term "You've Got Mail" may have been the most appealing noise your computer could make.

The term was so well branded it even became a movie title in 1998; **You've Got Mail** with Tom Hanks and Meg Ryan.*

I like to think that both of them are Limes...Meg Ryan for sure with her scrappy little bookstore!

Maybe it was the movie or maybe it was the 10 gazillion pieces of email spam that have hit inboxes around the world since...but the term, "You've Got Mail" has since lost its unopened-present-sitting-in-front-of-you reaction.

Nope. Today's email boxes are filled with messages about work, family, offers for discount Viagra, and the occasional notice of winning the multi-million-dollar lottery in some far off country you never heard of.

That said, despite the apparent email burn out, email marketing can be a big boost for your company...if done right (and no, you don't need a big list for some big results!).

Before I get into some strategies and tactics that worked great when email marketing, let's go over a couple rules about email marketing.

Rule #1 – Only send emails to people that have asked to receive them.

Don't be a @%&!. Don't be a spammer.

Aside from the fact that you will, at some point, get cut off from your Internet provider, people will just not like you. And if they don't like you, they won't do business with you. Period.

So, only send emails to those that want them from you.

The term is called "Permission Marketing."

That means the person has given his or her consent.

In the List Building chapter, I spoke about the Double Opt-in; where the person had to "confirm" that they wanted to receive your emails. That keeps your list pretty bulletproof – everyone wants your email.

Rule #2 – Don't send out too many emails.

Every once in a while I get on a list where someone feels the need to send out emails too frequently.

They are usually people that get some sort of "sale" off the email. I guess they figure if they send out more and more, they will get more money. In reality, they get people opting out of their list.

Don't get me wrong, they may get more money in the beginning just by beating people up. But what is the Lifetime Value of a customer? THAT is what you want!

Unless I signed up for a DAILY horoscope or DAILY stock notification, I don't want emails on a daily basis from anyone.

Granted, it really depends on who your audience is and the material you are delivering, but for the most part, I think once per week is plenty.*

Sometimes twice if you have something super cool to tell me that couldn't wait until next week.

Rule #3 – Don't send Cats instead of Dogs

Don't send information that is not relevant to the list (the reason they signed up in the first place).

For example, if I have built a list out of people that love cats, I am not going to send them an offer on dog supplies.

They are cat people. They didn't sign up for info on dogs, parrots, discount sporting goods, or saving money on car insurance. Give them what they want; cat stuff.

I see this time and time again.

Somebody has an email list full of a particular niche and then they send something completely irrelevant.

Once again, this leads to confusion and people opting out of your list.

Rule #4 – Don't only sell.

Even if someone signs up for your email marketing, you need to always provide value.

If all you ever do is ask for money or try and sell something, people will stop opening your emails and, you guessed it, opt-out.

Personally, I like to see 4-5 emails going out that contain content (no sales pitch) per one (1) sales email.

Now, of course there are some exceptions. You may have a business that doesn't make sense in sending pure "content."

For example, if you have a bakery that makes cupcakes, you are probably not going to send info about how to bake cupcakes.

But then again…why not?

Let's just say you email your database a recipe on how to make a certain cupcake.

How many people are going to go through all the trouble of making the cupcake versus how many people are going to just come in and buy the cupcake (since now they are thinking about it)?

You would be surprised how the more information and content you share, the more you sell. Totally counterintuitive, but it works!

Ok, now that we have a few ground rules set, let's get on to the fun part.

Creating a Kick Butt email Marketing Campaign

There is no "one size fits all" when it comes to creating a great email marketing campaign.

There are some basic items I like to stick to in a sales email campaign.

There needs to be some sort of benefit. Is it a discount? Is it a new item? Is it only available for a limited time? Is there a special guest?

Is there a way to send an email, going for some sort of sale, but still look good in the process?

The answer is "YES."

The following examples are for "sales" emails.

Although every company is a bit different, here are a couple "go to" strategies that have a tendency of working well.

The $100 Hammer for $4.25

This is the obvious one. It is simply an email that tells people what you have for sale. It usually needs a good discount, while keeping it short.

The sale is in the discount. Something like this:

Subject: Cupcake Wars

Greetings!

As you may know, we have been voted the #1 cupcake baker in Los Angles three years in a row!

And now we are going for FOUR!

Bring in this email in the <u>next 48 hours</u> and get $20 worth of cupcakes for only $5!

Really, we are not crazy, it is just our way of thanking our customers and what better way to "give back" than give cupcakes?

Really, no tricks, $20 worth of cupcakes for only $5.

See you soon,

Susie Cupcake III

There are no real "tricks" in this email. I call it the "hammer" because only one part works: what is the deal. Make it attractive and make it have a time limit!

It is such an incredible discount that the reader has to take action (no one likes to miss out on a deal if they can help it)!

This deal has an attractive price and creates urgency (only 48 hours).

Clean. Easy. Effective.

It also creates good will with your customers. You are celebrating and sharing the love!

Three Question Survey

I wish I could take credit for this one, but I can't. I learned this one awhile back from someone else and I improved upon it with some specialized web forms built just for the technique. The essence of it works great in an email campaign.

Here is what you need to do.

1. Create a survey on SurveyMonkey.com or one of the other free survey locations.

2. Do not make the survey longer than 3 questions.

3. After they have finished the survey, take them to a web page that thanks them for helping you out and offers them something for the trouble.

The questions of the survey are really irrelevant. I mean, make them something relevant to your business, but the survey is really just an excuse to send an email.

The beauty of this technique is that you don't look like you are "selling" anything, just asking for some help on a survey that will take less than a minute.

This is an example of just how short your email could be...

Subject: Can you help me?

Greetings!

*I was wondering if you could spare
60 seconds and answer three questions
for me.*

*I promise they are really easy, but it
will help me better serve you in the future.*

*Heck, I will even make it worth your while
and I promise it will only take 60 seconds.*

Quicklink→ Go Here (link)

All the best,

Daniel Marris

That is it. I might throw in a PS, but I certainly wouldn't make the body of this email any longer.

The longer the email the longer the person thinks the survey will be.

After they take the survey, the will get a page that says, "Hey, thanks for answering the survey, it will really help me out."

As a token of my appreciation, print this page for a [free appetizer, cup of coffee, cupcake, consulting session, car wash upgrade – whatever you want to offer].

123

You can even offer the same cupcake deal. The point is, the only reason they are getting the deal is because they helped you on the survey.

Important note: This technique needs to be reserved for very good deals, otherwise the person feels slighted. Put your best offer in this format, not just a 5% off.

Ta da! Pretty cool huh? Play your cards right and you can even do something with those survey answers.

The Results Are IN! (Three Question Survey...part two).

Hey, remember that survey we ran...oh...one example ago? Let's do something with it, like send out an email to our database.

Subject: I could not believe the results

Greetings!

Wow. When I asked my friends to take a short survey I had no idea the results and comments I would get.

All this time I never realized how important XXX was to my customers.

So...

You talked. I listened.

*Print out this email and redeem for
[insert whatever they redeem it for here]*

Thanks again!

Skippy Milson

In this case you can decide whether to send the email only to those that actually took the survey or everyone (just modify the text).

People love results. They want to see if they somehow influenced the survey with their own opinion.

It's "In The News"

It is always great when you can tie an email to a current event.

Local newspapers and the national news cover so many topics, at some point they are bound to overlap with your industry. Check out Google Alerts to help you keep current events related to your subject matter on your radar.

Here is an example of a current event email being able to be used for your own gain.

Subject: USA Today Names Biggest Investor Mistakes

I am sure by now you have heard about the shocking report USA Today did about the average stock market investor and HUGE mistakes they are making.

If you didn't, you can see the report here (link)

As a financial advisor, my entire day is devoted to not only helping people build a solid financial future...but also a solid "present."

For additional tips and strategies that I think USA Today forgot to add, check out this page On my site (link)

All the best,

Steven Rock

The news report can be in any form. If it was a video, I would actually go through the trouble of embedding the video on your own personal website (if allowed). This gets people to your site.

The trick to this technique is an inferred third party verification of what you have been saying all along gets you more (and new) business almost every time.

Action Items.

You know, the kind of thing Limes work on:

- Draft a "$100 Hammer" email

- Draft a "Three Question Survey" email (and the survey questions)

- Draft an "In the News" email

- Download the Email Cheat Sheet at BeTheLime.com/CheatSheets

BE THE LIME

Chapter Fourteen:

WHAT EMAIL MARKETING SERVICE SHOULD I USE?

"For email, the old postcard rule applies. Nobody else is supposed to read your postcards, but you'd be a fool if you wrote anything private on one."

– Judith Martin (Miss Manners*)*

Just about every business today needs to have some sort of "online" marketing campaign that utilizes emails or e-letters to communicate with current or prospective customers.

As your business grows and is more on target with respect to marketing, you are going to quickly outgrow the "manual" email send from your own computer and need to use an email marketing service.

Think of the service as a place to have all your customers' email information in one place, handy templates to help you create nice looking emails, and a host of tools to help spread the word of your business to others.

There are three big reasons you need to convert your email database to an email marketing service.

1. Email Deliverability

The fact of the matter is that if you keep emailing lots of people from your own personal computer, your current email provider will most likely shut you down at some point.

Even if they continue to allow you to send, the receiving person's ISP (Internet Service Provider) might start identifying the email as [bulk] spam and not even deliver them to your intended recipient.

2. Email Analytics

This goes way beyond "open" and "click through rates."

There are some very impressive strategies you can implement once you are working with an email service such as the ones listed below.

State of the art software lets you:

- Separate list
- Create sub-lists
- Create different messages for different types of prospects
- Create a follow up sequence to new people or "upsell" emails to those that have already taken action

3. Backup

All of your prior emails to your database, not to mention the database itself, is backed up off-site.

So, what email marketing services should you use?

First off, that is a pretty big question. A lot of it really depends on your budget and the features you must have. It is not uncommon to switch services as your needs grow.

So, in no particular order, here are the four most popular choices among our clients when it comes to email marketing services.

Special Note: Email marketing providers change their service offerings often. It is always best to check out the company's site directly for current pricing and features.

1. MailChimp

MailChimp is a great choice if you are just starting out...testing the waters so to speak. It is probably the most popular service of choice for our new or smaller clients (particularly in the beginning).

Pros

- MailChimp is the only major provider to offer a free account. There is no charge for MailChimp if you have fewer than 2,000 subscribers and are sending fewer than 12,000 emails per month. If you get above that, they offer upgraded plans that are still fairly priced.
- Wide range of templates to choose from (over 400).
- Easy to use dashboard (drop and drag)
- Editable "From" name on emails.
- Upload an existing list of contacts.

Cons

- MailChimp has limitations with regard to autoresponders at the free level (but fully functional with paid upgrade).
- They do not allow you to send one campaign to multiple subscriber lists.
- Somewhat "cheaper" market perception (but most likely only from those in the know...not your subscribers).

2. Aweber

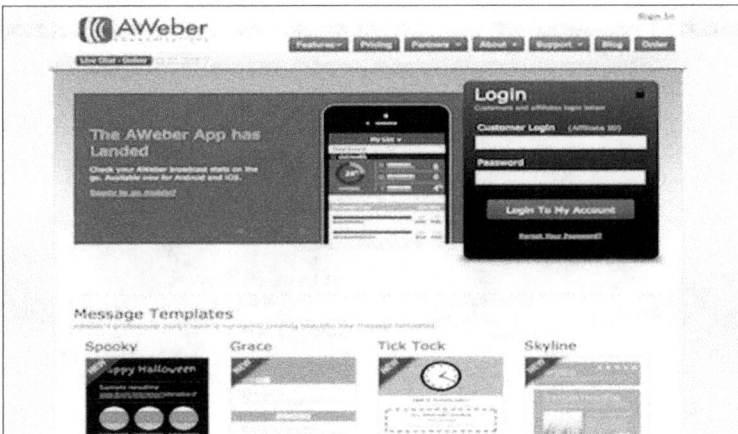

Aweber was one of the first ones I worked with of any magnitude. Although they have fallen behind in a few features, I still have many lists that I still run on Aweber.

Pros

- Over 150 templates to choose from
- Integrates easily with PayPal, WordPress, Eventbrite, and more.

- Editable "From" name on emails.
- Easily search lists and create "segments" based on actions.
- Good autoresponder features.
- Outstanding support

Cons

- A bit cumbersome to use "tagging" feature.
- No "Survey" function

3. Constant Contact

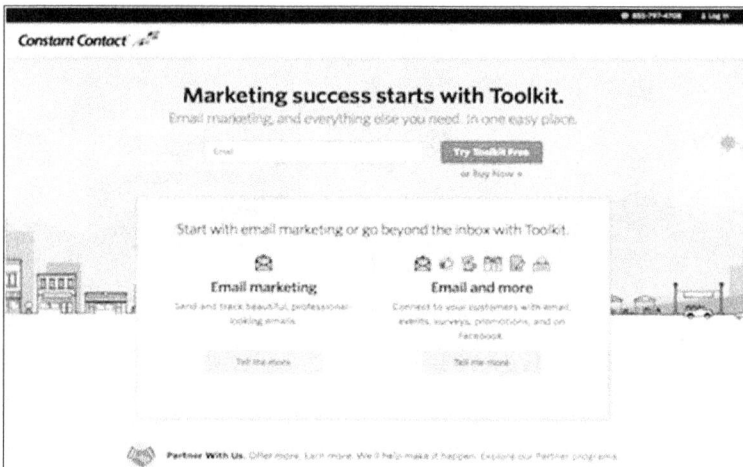

Probably one of the more popular email marketing services, Constant Contact is a favorite among small and medium sized businesses.

Pros

- Over 400 templates
- WordPress plug in as well as a Facebook "Fan Page" app.

- Editable "From" name on emails.
- Great analytics including complaints, opt-outs, click-through rates, and social shares.

Cons

- Additional fee to send survey to contacts.
- No free version for small-scale businesses ($20/mo. Starter package).

4. InfusionSoft

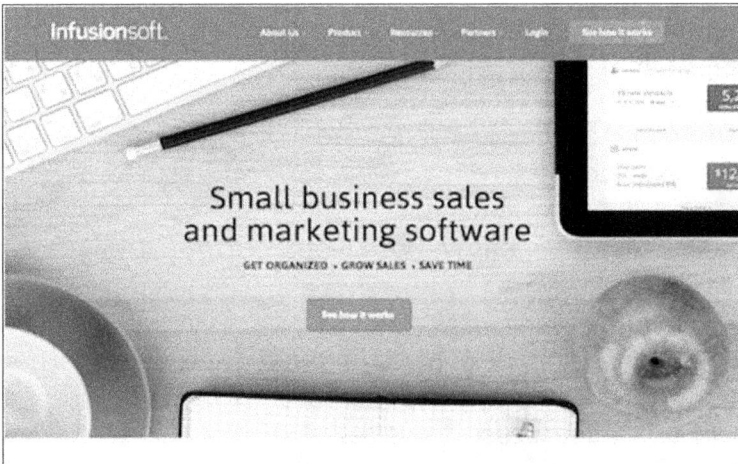

In some ways, InfusionSoft is the Rolex of email marketing. I mean, we are talking dreamy! It is virtually a one-stop shop toy store for email marketing. It also comes with a pretty hefty price.

Pros

- A full CRM system
- Email, social marketing, and e-commerce solutions.

- Detailed subscriber records.
- Unprecedented list segmentation and targeting.

Cons

- Price. Lowest tier starts at $199 a month for 2,500 contacts and 12,500 emails (sent per month).
- Not as user-friendly as other systems. With power, comes confusion, so expect a bit more of a learning curve.

So, now what?

Choosing an email marketing service can be a bit challenging.

It is helpful to know both your current and future plans.

That said, you can always move over to another service later if your business grows or needs additional features. However...

Moving a list from one service to another can be a hassle. Oftentimes, the new service will require you to have each of your users "re-confirm" their subscription.

Needless to say, typically there are a significant percentage of people that will not bother confirming (and thereby "drop" off your list). Something to consider when you move a list.

Action Items.

You know, the kind of thing Limes work on:

- Not sure who to pick? Feel free to hit me up online and tell me a little bit about your project. I will do my best to point you in the right direction.

BE THE LIME

Chapter Fifteen:

FACEBOOK - WE ARE THE PRODUCT

"Oh look, they all thought they were famous."

– Aliens finding Earth in the year 3016

Asking if I like Facebook is kind of asking if I wanted to be popular in High School.

I know that it would have been cool to get all that attention, but then again, I would have to hang out with people that go along with that.

Want to go to the Prom?

To me, the success of Facebook is largely due to people getting to re-live their high school popularity endeavors.

Most people on Facebook will tell you that they are only on it to "Re-connect with old friends." I am sure that may have been the intent, but after that first week – mission accomplished – Facebook turns into a whole other animal.

Look at me, I have 248 million "friends." "Oh, I got 14 likes on my status update, I feel so validated."

Now before you think I am getting too preachy about Facebook...

I have a Facebook account as well. I am guilty of posting narcissistic photos, one liners I find entertaining (if only to myself), and yes, enjoy it when people comment, post, or share.

So, I am speaking from the first phase of what could be a 12-step Facebook program. So, before I get hate mail, understand that I am calling myself out just as much as anyone else.

Under all those kittens videos...

Facebook has its pros and cons (and kittens).

Frankly you need to get through the top layer of superficial "please like me" phase to find its true business potential.

But, underneath that thin layer of "Monday sucks" and hundreds of Instagram photos of food lies a real market for those that are willing to hang in there.

So, if you dare, let's look at three big things that make Facebook attractive to almost every business or brand (large or small).

1. WE are the product.

With a lot of companies, the product is, well, an actual product. You know, cookies, computers, stuffed animals, an online training. Something tangible to hand off to someone else.

With Facebook, WE are the product.

The amount of information Facebook has is staggering. It would certainly drive any George Orwell followers to run & scream their way off the grid as fast as possible.

That said, it is a gold mine for anyone that is trying to promote a business or brand.

2. Free!

Hey, "free" has to be one of the most attractive things I could have possibly led with.

I mean sure, you are looking for results, but how many results do you need if it didn't cost you anything to begin with?

With the exception of paying for advertisements on Facebook, the cost to set up your account is zero. NO COST for a personal account, NO COST for a business fan page.

You can't watch a show on prime time without seeing some sort of Facebook icon show up (although I really think Twitter is winning the war on that front). Apparently we are supposed to drop what we are doing and head to the computer to go to the Facebook page.

A basic rule of marketing your business or brand is looking for ways to get your message in front of a lot of targeted people – for a low cost. Facebook passes that test.

3. Interaction.

Let's face it. People on Facebook talk...a lot.

When you post something on Facebook (a post, photo, link, whatever) you are bound to get some sort of feedback in a real hurry (assuming people have "friended*" you of course.)

*I am not even sure that "friended" is a real word.

Anyway, people who converse on Facebook are quick to respond, like, and share a post they find worthy of their attention. I am not sure I know a medium that has so much immediate interaction.

It tells me that a lot of people have a lot of time on their hands.

Side Note: I have heard the average Facebook user spends up to 50 minutes a day on Facebook. With only 24 hours in a day and the average time sleep, not mine, is 8.8 hours: That means 1/16 of the average waking hours are on Facebook.

Also, all interactions are archived ina way that you always see them. This keeps the conversation going, which is especially helpful for people in other time zones.

So, with Free and Interactions all lined up and ready to go, what is the best way for a business to get involved?

First off, a Fan Page.

You are going to want to go Facebook.com and set up Fan Page.

Here are a couple things that can really make your fan page shine.

Timeline cover photo

A lot of people were upset with Facebook when they changed everything to the "Timeline" format. Personally, I thought it worked well for businesses.

You have a [very] large cover photo that allows you to give the viewer an idea of who they are dealing with.

There is also a smaller profile photo (your avatar if you will) that will follow you throughout any comments you leave.

If you want something a bit more fancy, check out some turn-key themes out there for some ideas or simply pay someone to design one for you.

Invite Friends

In Facebook you can invite any "Friends" to your business account you may have tied to your personal Facebook account.

This can be a great way to get started. But...

Please don't be that person who invites everyone over to their house for a BBQ but then starts selling them magnets (I got stuck at a BBQ like that once).

In other words, try and really think about which friends it might be appropriate to invite. Your friends can be a very supportive...but only to a point before you start sending them stuff you know they could care less about.

So, now what?

Now that you have a Fan page the real magic can begin. But let me start with a couple facts you need to be aware of.

Let's say you have 200 people that have "Liked" your new business fan page, "Cupid's Cupcakes."

When you post something, that means that up to

200 people *could* see it on their wall.

The fact of the matter is that maybe 30% will see it out of the gate, if you are lucky.

Facebook does not serve your post to every person who likes your page. Now, if the 60 people find it interesting (leave comments, likes, etc) you may start hitting a higher percentage of walls.

So delivering interesting and relevant posts should always be at the top of your list.

What should you post?

In this case, a pic of a cupcake would be a great start. But non-stop cupcake posting would get really old, which means fewer interactions and fewer people seeing your posts over time.

What would I post if I had a cupcake business (keeping in mind that I know nothing about the cupcake business except that they taste good)? Off the top of my head:

- ✓ The occasional cupcake (something that looks great and has a story).
- ✓ Some cute kid eating a cupcake. The messier the better – frosting all over the face. Parent permission is a must.
- ✓ Someone famous, or locally famous, eating a cupcake. Firemen and Policemen are also great.
- ✓ Pic of some raw ingredients with the caption "Dreaming of being a cupcake."
- ✓ Cupcake pic (special on sale)

✓ Outside of the building with some catchy phrase like, "Through these doors, dreams are made true."

✓ A cupcake recipe (no one will take the time to make it...but they will think you are really cool for sharing it).

You will notice that only one of the seven had anything to do with directly selling a cupcake.

Why?

Because they get it.

They **know** you want to sell cupcakes. You don't need to hammer them over the head with it.

Facebook is about staying on their mind.

By sharing things that don't scream "BUY ME" they will continue to follow you—and buy cupcakes.

The other thing you will notice is I have chosen items I think people will either "share," "like," or "comment" on.

That is key and very helpful for a business wanting to grow on Facebook.

If someone "shares" your posts on their wall, that is an automatic inferred third-party credibility piece.

Now, let's say that #2 starts taking off. I mean really, who doesn't like a messy kid photo? The next thing I would do is "Boost Post."

What is "Boosting" a post?

Boosting a post is kind of like an ad, but you have a lot less control (it is also a lot cheaper).

These are good for branding and will go to your fans and their friends.

For $10 you might have it show up on 2500 walls.

When we do Facebook advertising for a client, we run a mix of Boost Posts and Facebook Ads.

Granted the lions share is in paid ads, but the Boost Post can deliver some great home runs when managed correctly. *So much so, that the potential view can far exceed the number of fans you have!*

What about Advertising on Facebook?

I am, at least right now, a big fan of Facebook advertising. You can promote a page, posts, or even a website (off Facebook).

I do want to mention that you can place an advertisement with the intent of gaining more "likes." This can help build the audience of people that see your posts.

Be sure to read the "Advertising" chapter because you are going to want a Facebook ad geared towards getting likes to be very targeted.

You can also use contest formats (such as Rafflecopter) to promote your page and gain more likes (and traffic).

Oh, and one more thing.

There is no doubt an all-out battle on social media for real-time action.

Facebook has launched something called Facebook Live and this could be a game changer for a lot of businesses and brands.

Now, as the name "live" name might suggest, it is video. So you have to be comfortable getting in front of the camera or filming something live (the camera does not need to be pointed at yourself).

Soon as I wrap up this book I will be sure to put some posts on <u>BeTheLime.com</u> to give you a jump start!

Action Items.

You know, the kind of thing Limes work on:

- Set up a Personal Facebook account

- Set up a Business Fan Page

- Create an Avatar and main photo for each page

- Add one or two posts per day

- Once set up, invite friends to "Like" your business page

- Boost a post or two (not on the same day)

- Consider a running a targeted ad to gain more likes

BE THE LIME

Chapter Sixteen:

A BIRD IN THE HAND IS WORTH?

*"I don't do Twitter because
I don't want to talk about myself
more than I already have to."*

- Kit Harington.

When a company, business, or individual comes to our firm for help, we usually have an initial "meeting" to see what their objectives are and if we are a good fit.

For whatever reason, Twitter seems to be one of the most misunderstood social media platforms out there, and yet, one of the most popular.

Almost every prospective client thinks they want to be on Twitter. No, they NEED to be on Twitter (they heard it from a friend).

The fact of the matter is Twitter really doesn't work for 8 of 10 businesses. The main reason is that Twitter is GLOBAL, not necessarily local.

If you are building your brand on a national (or global) basis, by all means, Tweet on. Otherwise it might just be a big waste of time.

I am not trying to dissuade you from Twitter, I use it everyday. I just want to use this moment as a reminder you don't have to be involved in every social media fad out there.

Some social media platforms will be great fits for your business.

For others, the extent of your actions will be going out, registering your user name, and maybe an occasional "check in" or post.

So why does everyone want to be on Twitter?

By now, you see Twitter everywhere.

Watch the morning news and you will see a variety of newscaster's Twitter names flash on the screen. @JoeMorningNewsCaster or something like that.

Hot topic? They will put the Hashtags on the screen

#TwinkiesComeBack

At night you will find them on any reality show or special.

Yep, Twitter has done a great job piercing the market.

But does it fit you? Why are so many businesses really interested in Twitter?

I think it is that Rock Star perception. I mean if a @YokoOno can get 4.7 million followers it shouldn't be hard for me to get some right?

And, if I get some followers, that could mean business!

But what exactly is Twitter?

You remember that game as a child when you tied two cans together via a piece of string?

You know the one that had you shouting into a can and the vibrations ran down the length of the can until reaching the person on the other end (who could then "hear" you no thanks to the fact you were only 10 feet away to begin with?).

Well, Twitter is kind of like that, except sometimes, despite your talking, there is no one on the other end.

Or, even worse, there are 7 billion cans & strings and you can't separate the "noise" from the good stuff.

IF, and that is a big "if," Twitter is right for your type of business, you may find it good for...

....keeping in touch with fans
...announcing new things
...running a last minute test or "special"
...publically taking care of some bad PR
...gain insight to your customers and how to better serve them

Like many of the other social media sites in this book I am going to tell you to set up a Twitter account even if you don't end up using it. Jello locked up their twitter name (@Jello) even if they don't really seem to do anything with it.

Setting up your account is easy. Go to Twitter.com and create an account.

The account is going to be tied to an email and Twitter will send you a confirmation email that you must click on to complete the setup.

At the time of this writing, Twitter was still limiting your **User Name** to 15 characters. So if you were hoping for @BradIsTheCoolestTwitterUserEver, you are going to have to tone it down a bit.

If you can find a Twitter user name that matches your company name, great. More often than not, you are going to have to be a bit creative.

Keep in mind that you can create more than one account per entity. One for your business, one for you personally.

At some point in your future, your personal twitter account may take over (especially if YOU become the brand). For example, I have twitter account for most of my companies, but the bulk of my tweets are sent via my personal account, @Godfadr.

You can see that, very early on, I did not push @ExposureOne or even @BeTheLime in favor of @Godfadr.

However, I still need a place for those people that only know about Exposure One to go – I mean @Godfadr is a pretty big disconnect if you don't know my Twitter name and the reason for it.

The @TwitterName will always stay the same, but you can change the "title" if you wish.

Most of what you see on Twitter will show both lines simultaneously. For example:

You Can Change This Title (Name up to 20 characters)
@Twitter Name (Username up to 15 characters)

So, try and find something close to your company name, even a short version of it.

I tend to make the "name" line the same unless the company is so broad the title needs clarification or we couldn't get close enough on the Twitter name.

Now that you are set up on Twitter, should you actually start tweeting and opening up that floodgate?

Let's look at a few things that may help you determine if using Twitter is a good fit.

Psst. I think you are being followed.

Twitter is a made of up of people following each other, but in less of a creepy stalker way.

When you "follow" someone, you are going to see what he or she has to say (in the form of Tweets).

You decide which people you follow and which you don't.

Just because someone is following you it doesn't mean you are going to want to follow them.

For the most part, you DO NOT decide who follows you.*

Although if you ever don't like someone following you, you can "Block" him or her at any time.

So, you have to be interesting enough for people to follow you.

They are basically saying, "Whatever you talk about (via Tweets) is going to show up on my feed."

Now, just because someone is following you, doesn't mean they see your tweets on any consistent level.

If a person follows 500 people who all happen to be tweeting around the same time, your post will probably get lost on his or her "feed."

So, just because you have followers, it doesn't mean each one will see every message you post. But that also doesn't mean you shouldn't keep on the radar of the ones that are paying attention to what you say.

Uh oh. Are you long winded?

Here is example of a Twitter post...

Twitter posts are a max of 140 characters. If you are long winded or like to wax poetic on each of your tweets, you will be cut off, most li..

See what I mean. It is tough.

There is an art to writing short "Tweets" that both convey a message and prompt a response. Although some people get into a considerable amount of abbreviations, most do not, so plan on getting pretty witty with the short prose.

On the plus side, a portion of your tweets can link to a webpage or blog post you have elsewhere. Something like...

"We are going to change everything you know about cookies for 48 hours [LINK]."

Not only is it well within the 140-character limit, it does raise an eyebrow and beg to be clicked. FYI : Links are abbreviated in Twitter, so you won't lose the use of too many characters if you have a long url link.

Are you ready to talk...a lot?

There are basically three ways someone tries to get your attention in Twitter. Using the "@YourName," Direct Messaging (DM's) and #Hashtags.

#1 - @YourName

Tweeting @YourName looks like:

"Had a great time with @Godfadr" last night at the soccer game."

For the most part, that is a passive tweet. It will show up in your "@ Mentions" wall. You can choose to respond or not – one is not necessarily expected.

The other type of name tweet could be a specific question like:

"@Godfadr, are you going to the soccer game tonight?"

That tweet requests some sort of response or I risk losing the follower.

I have been asked a specific question that I need to answer with something like...

"@TheirUserName You bet. Will see you there right after the radio interview"

#2 – Direct Message (DM)

If that wasn't enough, there is another way for people to get a hold of you on Twitter (although less frequent).

It is called "Direct Message" or DM for short.

Think of DM just like an email inbox.

The only person that gets the DM is you. On the plus side, it is a great way to take a public Twitter conversation to a private venue.

One downside it is yet another email box to monitor. The other problem is the DM box seems be a favorite among spammers and hackers (although it has been a lot better lately).

#3 - Hashtags

Hashtags are a great way to search twitter or create a thread based on a subject rather than a tweet. For example:

"Who's going to the #WineFest?"

"@name can't wait for the #WineFest Monday night!"

"@name New vendor slots for #WineFest. Call us!"

"#WineFest is on people. Tickets on Sale NOW!"

With #Hashtags, every one of those tweets would show up in a search *(if I searched for #WineFest whether I follow them or not).*

Hashtags are great for what is trending or most talked about on Twitter. There are also some fun strategies for using hashtags on a day-to-day campaign.

IF Twitter is a good move for you and/or your business, you are going to have to realize it will take a significant portion of your time, especially as your popularity grows.

That said, I don't want to scare you...

By now you are probably ready to run away as far as you can from Twitter so let me rope a few of you back in.

In some instances, and businesses, Twitter is invaluable.

When I was starting a cigar company called Nomad, Twitter was instrumental in communicating with cigar smokers, fans, reviewers, and writers.

I found a whole passionate community tweeting about what cigar they were smoking, what they liked, and what they didn't.

It led me to launching the cigar brand with the Twitter user name right on the outside of the band (something no other cigar company had ever done).

Twitter was no doubt a major influence on the fast growing popularity of the cigar line.

So, what is the bottom line on "IF" you should be on Twitter?

Will you have ongoing conversations with your fans and potential customers that goes beyond the scope of just selling them stuff?

Zagg makes protective film covers for iPhones, computers, cameras, etc. @Zaggdaily is their Twitter account user name (they could not get @Zagg as it was already taken).

They really only have one goal:

Get you to buy a screen protector. But, the bulk of their tweets are about cell phones, computers, surveys, viral videos.

They understand that they will not be able to keep their followers if all they are doing is pitching their stuff.They need to provide value.

If you are going to have an active twitter account, you need to have value beyond just trying to sell your followers things.

Although there is no hard and fast rule, I like to see at least 15 non-sale related tweets for every one self-promotional tweet.

Personally, I like Twitter for some of my clients, but certainly not all. I would guess that an active Twitter account is really only useful for about 20% of all businesses (but very powerful for those 20%).

See what your competitors are doing on twitter.

- ✓ Can you emulate or do better?
- ✓ If they don't have an audience...why don't they?

✓ Do they have lots of users that you can follow?

Twitter is about ongoing, but brief, conversations. Snapshots in time; but those snapshots could yield you big returns, raving fans, and a new source of income.

Action Items.
You know, the kind of thing Limes work on:

- Set up an account with Twitter. Choose your UserName carefully as it cannot be changed.

- Set @ tweets and DM's on your account to text message you or email you. That way you don't have to log on to your account all the time to see if you have a message.

- Be sure to upload a photo. Otherwise you are stuck with the ugly Twitter "Egg" that just screams amateur.

- Look at a few programs that help you manage your twitter account. We list a few at BeTheLime.com/Resources. Programs can help you schedule tweets and find more people to follow.

- Looking for more followers? Check out

your competition. You can go to their Twitter account and see who they follow and who follows them.

- Pay attention to (Follow Friday) #FF if you see people on your feed doing this. This happens on, surprise, Friday. They are usually a recommendation from followers on other people you should be following. Oftentimes this list is a great source of finding new followers.

- Use hashtags in tweets when possible. For example, "Had a great cookie from @Oreo. #cookies #snacktime" – That tweet will be seen by followers and anyone that looks up "cookies" or "snacktime" on twitter. Great way to find people with common interests and many will end up following you!

BE THE LIME

Chapter Seventeen:

IS THIS FOOD INSTAGRAMABLE?

"It's like the food network...but with selfies."

\- Fred Rewey

I would be lying if I said I thought Instagram would be great for business in the beginning.

But, like any successful social media platform, success is defined by how many people are using it. The more people using it, the more successful it can be for a business.

What did I say in an earlier chapter? You go where the people are!

So...helloooooo Instagram.

For those catching up on, or not yet familiar with Instagram, it is pretty much exclusively served up on a smartphone and, unlike many of the other social media platforms, sticks to real-time posting.

Instagram is picture based.

In the beginning I would have sworn that Instagram was 85% pictures of Food, 10% of Sunsets, and the rest random buildings.

So, like Pinterest, you really want to have a business or a brand that is photo heavy. Or can at least create the appearance of such.

There are really two main goals when using Instagram.

- ✓ Increase traffic to your website
- ✓ Increase your brand awareness

Either one can be great but the platform itself can be a bit labor intensive and really does not provide direct selling (via links).

I will talk about Instagram Stories in a minute, but first let me pass on a few tips for your basic Instagram account.

✓ Like all social media accounts, try and procure a username (and look) that is close to your business or your brand. Something people will learn to recognize or seek out right away.

For Be_The_Lime I generally use this for my avatar..

Pretty basic right?

Yep, just a snapshot of a lime.

It is simply a screen shot (cut out) from the **Be the Lime Podcast** cover. So it does not need to be very complex.

✓ Even if you don't plan on using Instagram much (like me) then at least lock it down. It is not really how I market Be The Lime but I did make sure I got the username and threw up a few posts. Better me to have my brand than someone else!

✓ Use Hashtags - #Hashtags provide another way for people to find you in Instagram (as well as Twitter). Sometimes people will actually search for posts under a popular hashtag. If you used that hashtag in your post, people will find you. Just don't get to spammy and put dozens of hashtags in your comments.

✓ Post on a consistent basis. If you are just starting out, I would say to post twice a day to start.

✓ Until you know exactly when your audience is online, in addition to posting twice a day, I would vary the times that you post. Pay attention to when you get more "comments" or "likes" and gravitate towards posting at those times.

✓ Although I am not a big fan of sharing the same exact content across numerous social media platforms, sharing your Instagram posts on Facebook and Twitter can be a great way to get people to find your Instagram account (and then follow you). Instagram is not the easiest program to find your friends, so any bit helps.

✓ If you really start to get some traction, you might want to click on over to Instagram's Business Tools. With a business account, you'll get access to new business features and Instagram Insights.

- ✓ Be sure to fill out your profile and explain a little about yourself, your business, or your brand. This is also the place to reference your website. I am amazed at how many people overlook this.

- ✓ Follow others. If you follow other boards, comment and like theirs, you will find they start doing the same for your content.

So, if Instagram largely sounds like a Friday night slide show at Grandma's house, you are not far off...until...

Enter **Instagram Stories**.

Instagram Stories just might be a game changer on Instagram. Basically, Instagram Stories are a collection of photos (in a slideshow) and videos, all with a 24-hour expiration notice on them.

The can be made up of whatever you like and you can add lots of cute stuff like bubbles, text, and you can even add music in the background.

Oh, and no one can actually publicly like or comment on your story.

At any time, you can see who watched your story and if they want to interact, they actually RESPOND to you via a message. If you want, you can turn that setting off.

But, can you see how you now have meaningful interaction?

Action Items.

You know, the kind of thing Limes work on:

- Create an Instagram account with your phone

- Lock down a user name for you, your brand, or your business. Even if you don't plan on using it right now.

- Go back and read the "tips" in this chapter and get started!

- Oh yea, go follow @Be_The_Lime on Instagram. Maybe that will finally make me do something with it :)

Chapter Eighteen:

PINTEREST (AND REFRIGERATOR MAGNETS)

"Ask not what you can do for your country. Ask what's for lunch."

– Orson Welles

If Instagram is about food, then Pinterest is about crafts.

Let me start by saying if you are one of those people who has a refrigerator full of magnets to the point that you can no longer identify the color of your fridge, you are probably not going to be a happy with me for a moment.

When the owner of the bevy of magnets looks at the fridge, they see a series of vacations, birthdays, reunions, restaurants, amusing quotes, and various milestones all laid out in a beautiful mosaic.

I pretty much see a mess.

But, one person's mess is another person's kaleidoscope of discovery, and who am I to stand in the way of what seemingly seems to work for some people.

What does this have to do with Pinterest?

Pinterest is made up of lots of people who like refrigerator magnets, or at the very least bulletin boards.

Officially, Pinterest is a content sharing service that allows members to "pin" images, videos and other objects to their pinboard.

What seemed to start as a result of people sharing various crafts, recipes, and home remodeling tips, has now grown into a full-blown social media opportunity for some businesses.

How does it work?

Each member of Pinterest receives "Pinboards." On them, you can post whatever you like. You can share articles, videos, pictures—pretty much whatever you find around the web. You are allowed multiple Pinboards, so you will most likely separate them by category.

People who visit your Pins can see the items and "re-pin" them. Then the item shows up on their board.

Quick Note: It is very important to note that some numbers suggest that up to 80% of pins are RE-Pins (that is a lot of sharing!)

Can you see the benefit?

People may continue to share your pin if they feel there is value or want it on their pinboard as well, all the while maintaining credit back to you.

Everyone's home page will contain various pins from people they follow.

Oh yea, you choose who to follow – sound familiar?

So who is on Pinterest and what do they want to see?

In 2012 it was reported that 83% of the U.S. users were women. However, in Britain, 56% of the users were reported to be men with the average age of 35-44.

The Women...

As I mentioned before, Pinterest was embraced predominately by women in the beginning as a way to share crafts.

The top interests among U.S. women were...

Crafts
Gifts and Special Occasion Items
Hobbies
Fashion

You only need to go to the Pinterest home page (not logged in) to see that this trend is very much alive.

The Men...

The funny part of the male trend to Pinterest is that, at least at the time of this writing, the pins were still very much related back to women. The three most popular categories/boards were....

Things my wife should cook (food and more food)
Things I'd like my wife to wear (yep, pretty much lingerie).
Things my wife makes me wear (clothes).

That said, there are a few things (in the UK) that are trending among males...

Venture Capital, Blogging, Public Relations, Web Content, and Crafts.

What about "big brands?"

For the most part, big brands have avoided Pinterest unless they have something visually stimulating. Companies such as Whole Foods, Cooking Light, Williams-Sonoma, and Bon Appetit have all jumped on board (sorry, no pun intended).

Although that may change in the future, the site is still driven by look and feel, thus leaving some businesses out in the cold trying to figure out just how they might fit in.

Is Pinterest right for you and your business?

Here is one way to tell if Pinterest is right for you:

Do you have photos to share?

Certainly Pinterest is not limited to sharing photos (you can share blog posts, articles, etc), but photos are the major catalyst to items being quickly discovered or shared.

Text is not near as fun to throw up on the fridge, so viewing it on the Pinterest board is not going to work much either.

Now, you can cheat if you will. You can write a great article, add a photo and put text with it. Use that photo for your post and attract readers. But without a catchy photo it will probably be lost in the Pinterest world.

Are you in a hot category?

According to Repinly, at the time of this writing…

Top Boards

Food and Drink
Home Décor
Other
Art
Design
Women's Fashion
Photography
DIY & Crafts
Film, Music, & Books

Top Pins

Food and Drink
Other
DIY & Crafts
Home Décor
Women's Fashion
Hair and Beauty
Weddings
My Life, Kids, & Humor

If you have a business in any of those areas, you definitely want to give Pinterest a whirl.

Ready to start pinning? Here are four big tips...

1. Quotes and photos are worth money! *Be sure to add a link to your website!*

2. Don't just sell.People hate being sold all the time. What valuable information can you share (via pin) that your followers would also enjoy?

3. Don't stray too far. Just because you are sharing other information, don't stray too far from your central message or theme. Remember, if your business/board is about apples, too many posts about oranges will drive people away.

4. Check it out before you re-pin. Don't get too quick and start re-pinning items for your readers. Whatever you re-pin is also a reflection of you. Take the time to click through and see what the complete message is before you re-pin.

5. Whenever possible, create an *original* pin and link it back to your website.

Want more tips?

Would you believe there is even a Pinterest board on Pinterest tips? Yep...

http://pinterest.com/kanter/pinterest-tips-and-tricks/

So now what?

Ok Magnet Maven (or man), Pinterest is pretty visual and this is well...a book.

So go check out Pinterest for yourself and you will see in about five minutes whether you fit in or not. Of course, you will also kill the next two hours looking at motivational quotes, crafts, or art.

Action Items.

You know, the kind of thing Limes work on:

- Go out and create a Pinterest account.

- Look around your business. Are there interesting things you can take a picture of and "Pin?"

- What about your competition? What are they doing on Pinterest?

Chapter Nineteen:

SERIOUSLY? THEY STILL DO PRESS RELEASES?

"If you don't read the newspaper, you're uninformed. If you read the newspaper, you're mis-informed."

– Mark Twain

I wish they would bring back that scrappy kid standing on the street corner yelling, "Extra Extra, read all about it" as he passed out newspapers.

The most recent news being shouted across the road just commanded attention, and that kid was the catalyst.

To be honest, I am not old enough to remember any newspaper-hawking children, but I will be old enough to tell future generations what newspapers once were (in a time before the news is directly beamed to someone's head or something like that.)

Newspapers were filled with current events, scandals, advertisements, and stories.

There was a lot of pressure to "fill" a newspaper. I suspect there still is.

Pick up any newspaper today and just think of the amount of fresh content it takes to print that thing day in and day out.

Newspaper writers were desperate for information.

Enter the Press Release

One way to get "your story" printed in a paper was to issue what was called a Press Release.

Press Releases are short little bursts of news about you or your company. Sometimes they are printed just "as is" but sometimes they prompt an eager writer to write more – a full blown story even!

The best part is that the company's cost is relatively nothing. An advertisement costs money, an article does not. And yet, both can get you business.

I knew him, Horatio

The apparent death of the printed news does not stop the benefits of an actual Press Release.

Online news has taken its place. It is fast to get to "print" and can be shared with others with unprecedented speed.

Nowadays, releasing a Press Release is sometimes a shot in the dark as to how many online sites may pick it up, but when they do, you are looking at traffic you would have never otherwise found.

The Press Release can help market your business both locally and on the Internet. Here are some tips for writing an effective press release:

- ✓ Keep it short and to the point.

- ✓ Print the words, "For Immediate Release" in the top left hand margin.

- ✓ Be sure to include the most important info in the first paragraph (who, what, when, etc). Articles are cut from the bottom up.

- ✓ Include a "dateline" in the first line of body that includes where this is being released. For example: ORLANDO, FL – November 3, 2016.

181

✓ Press releases are written in third person using block style (not paragraph indentation).

✓ Quote from you.

✓ Tell the audience why information is intended for them and why they should continue to read it.

✓ Include these marks, "# # #" at the bottom to indicate the end of the press release.

✓ Be sure to include where the reader can get more information. A website is a great option to include.

✓ Do not include a photo unless it is both relevant and you have the rights to it.

✓ Keep the tone of the release all business. Do not include personal or non-business related details. This will often lead to the entire release not being posted.

The following examples contain several Press Release examples from PRLog (http://www.prlog .org/) and a template from http://www.free-press-release.com.

Be sure to visit them online to submit your press release for free distribution to Google news, multiple search engines, and thousands of RSS feeds.

You can also find some great gigs on Fiverr.com related to Press Releases. Some people will write them, other people will submit them for you.

If you're short on time, hire someone. Many worthwhile sites want a manual submission, not a computer program churning out press releases. Fiverrr.com is one of those companies, and it's some of the best money spent.

As I mentioned earlier, Press Releases are a little bit of a shot in the dark. I certainly don't think it needs to be a main part of your marketing, but, you should have a Press Release go out from time to time (one per month is a good goal).

Press Release Example from Free-Press-Release.com:

This Is Your Breath-Taking Headline, Within 100 Characters

A summary paragraph follows your headline. One or two sentences briefing the story are good.

For Immediate Release

City/State, Country (Free-Press-Release.com) - June 25, 2010 - A well-written leading sentence of 30 words or less works great to grab peoples' attention.

And here comes the detailed story. Keep them within 800 words and get rid of grammatical errors.

And here comes the detailed story. Keep them within 800 words and get rid of grammatical errors. And here comes the detailed story. Keep them within 800 words and get rid of grammatical errors. And here comes the detailed story. Keep them within 800 words and get rid of grammatical errors.

And here comes the detailed story. Keep them within 800 words and get rid of grammatical errors. And here comes the detailed story. Keep them within 800 words and get rid of grammatical errors. And here comes the detailed story. Keep them within 800 words and get rid of grammatical errors. And here comes the detailed story. Keep them within 800 words and get rid of grammatical errors.

The final paragraph restates the headline of news story together with the main newsworthy material.

About Company Ltd.
Include a short introduction to your company.
Phone number: 888-888-8888

Contact:
Your Name, director of PR
pr@company.com Company Ltd.
888-888-8888
http://www.Free-Press-Release.com

###

In 2012, I decided to turn another one of my hobbies into a business. I leveraged many of the things from this book, including press releases.

Soon after I launched the Nomad Cigar Company I saw a division in the industry about online tobacco sales. At the time, briefly, we were selling cigars online direct to customers.

I had planned on eventually taking online sales off our site at some point anyway – but a carefully worded Press Release put me in even better light and I received great traffic (and industry support) because of it.

Here is what I had for the Press Release...

Nomad Cigar Company Takes Stand with Retail Shops

For Immediate Release

Orlando, FL – September 01, 2012 – To show support for brick and mortar cigar shops, the Nomad Cigar Company has discontinued its direct to consumer online sales pages.

"Really, I never wanted the online portion of the business long term. It was necessary to get the word out about Nomad, particularly as a new boutique cigar maker, but now it is time to leave the cigars in the hands of shops around the nation that need to be supported." Said Fred Rewey, Nomad's Founder.

The move was not an easy one, especially for a start-up boutique cigar maker. In doing so, the Nomad Cigar Company temporarily loses customers that are not living near a brick and mortar location. Secondly, and perhaps most importantly, Nomad loses out on the profit that comes with direct online distribution.

"I am not going to lie, the profit of direct to consumer is nice – particularly for a new company. But, I have to look long term. My goal was not only to create a solid cigar; I wanted to also support the cigar industry as a whole. I believe this keeps things moving in the right direction." Rewey added. It is no surprise that as more and more cigar makers have supported sales online, Rewey's move, especially from a new

company, is music to the ears of some shops.
Rewey said, "Look, I think you need to have some sort of online sales for those customers that simply cannot get to a shop. But, the pricing does not need to be at the expense of local shops around the nation that bust their butts to create a great cigar smoking experience."

Those going to Nomad Cigar Company's "purchase page" are now greeted with a brief open letter from Rewey explaining his stance. Rewey is hoping for continued growth and Nomad's Cigars showing up in more and more retail shops.

Nomad Cigar Company was launched earlier this year with a well-received cigar and some groundbreaking innovations; such as Rewey putting his Twitter name (@Godfadr) on the cigar band.

He is hoping that his continued support of brick and mortar retail stores will help him grow his brand long term.

Interested retailers can contact the company directly for info on pricing, cigars, etc..

Contact:
Nomad Cigar Company
Fred Rewey
Twitter: @Godfadr
Phone: 855-MYNOMAD (or 855-696-6623)
Godfadr@NomadCigarCompany.com
http://www.NomadCigarCompany.com

#

In looking back, that Press Release was a bit long, but it received a tremendous about of press that helped get the business even more attention.

Your Press Release

Chances are, you have something going on at least monthly such as...

- ✓ New Sales Record
- ✓ New Product
- ✓ Limited or Seasonal Product
- ✓ Special Event
- ✓ Special Guest
- ✓ New Employee
- ✓ New Client

Once you get going, you can see the list goes on and on.

No matter which strategies you pick in this book, Press Releases should be a part of your plan. They are fast, inexpensive, and can yield some good results.

Action Items.

You know, the kind of thing Limes work on:

- Take a look the press release templates.

- Look for Press Releases from other companies in your industry.

- Write one Press Release about something new in your company.

- Consider using a ghostwriter off places like Fiverr.com for your first attempt.

- Start keeping a list of those that print (or write) about what you put out in a Press Release. Those should be your "A" players you pay more attention to.

Chapter Twenty:

VIDEO MARKETING YOUR WAY TO STARDOM!

"You don't have to be naked to be sexy."

– Nicole Kidman

Admit it. The movie was better.

I know, people always say, "the book was so much better" but was it?

Come on. Really better?

I get it. There are two schools of thought here.

On one side, when reading a book you get to "picture" all those people in your head. The surroundings, the characters, the sights and smells - all created in that grey matter between your ears.

On the movie side, you get rocked out of your seat by a sound system as you are visually attacked for two hours on a two-story screen. Oh, and there is a $1,700 bucket of popcorn!

Better yet...

Would you rather read about how to cook an amazing intricate pastry to serve your friends or would you rather see a video of a chef, showing you step-by-step, how to make it flawlessly?

I rest my case. Video is cool, better, and fun.

But I don't want to be on camera...

Before we get too far in this idea and some people bail because they don't want to be in front of the camera, let me say this:

"You don't have to be in front of a camera to create a successful video marketing campaign."

Sure, it helps depending on your objective, but there are many creative ways to create a video without being in front of the camera. Tools such as Screen Capture and Power Point are just a couple.

So don't dismiss the possibility of video marketing just because you are in a witness protection program and can't be seen by super villains that are still trying to find you!

First off...what is your objective?

There are two different ways (or terms) when it comes to creating videos for marketing. Are you...

1. Marketing WITH Video? or
2. Marketing A Video?

Although the difference between the two is subtle, it is worth mentioning before you start out on creating a video.

In Marketing WITH Video, you are usually selling somethingspecific.

It is a sales video.

It features your product and shows the viewer what it is, how they can use it, why they need it, and where they can get it.

Marketing a Video is generally trying to build brand awareness...

...even if that "brand" is you.

This type of video is often about giving information, educating people if you will.

Taken to an extreme, the latter can be one that is shared from one person to another; a stand-alone piece that can sometimes, if you are very lucky, go viral.

There is no wrong or right. As a matter of fact, you will probably look to do both at one point or another.

It is just important to know from the beginning what your objective is and not get stuck in-between the two.

Ready to be the next online Steven Spielberg? Let's start with some ideas!

The challenge with video is often not knowing where to start.

What should you say?
What is the goal of the video?
Why would someone want to watch this?
What is the expected outcome of someone watching the video?

Well, here are few base ideas that can be excellent jumpstarts for a video in any industry or on any topic...

- ✓ **Educate** – Teach people something about your product or service.

- ✓ **Do a Review** – Did someone release something in your industry you can review?

This is an excellent way to talk about something that will give you credibility and potentially circle back around to you and your product.

- ✓ **Case Studies** – Do you have actual "deals" or "case studies" you can share? People love real life examples.

- ✓ **Answer Questions** – Do you get asked questions about your product or service? Create a video that answers the "Top 5 Questions" about X.

- ✓ **Disprove Myths** – People love it when you shoot at some myths or outright misinformation. Set the record straight and you could have a whole new group of passionate followers.

- ✓ **Tell a Story** – People love stories (especially in video). Do you have something to share? If so, someone will want to hear it!

Some Video Creation Tips.

When creating videos, here are a couple "tips" that can help them spread around the web a bit easier.

- ✓ **Pay attention to your video's title.** The title of your video is almost as powerful as the video itself. Spend time thinking of a good title. Imagine looking at a list of tabloid headlines at the grocery check out line. The title of your video is your headline. Why should I tune in? Did you "sell me" from the start?

✓ **The videos need to have good content.** You don't need professional lighting and a killer sound system, but you do need to give out good information. Solid information will trump production quality every time. Nowadays you can shoot just about anything for the web on an iPhone.

✓ **Sound is key.** As I mentioned above, people will put up with poor lighting and a few other glitches in exchange for solid content. It is however difficult to get around poor sound quality. It might be worth a few bucks to invest in a good microphone or have someone do a post-video audio clean up.

✓ **Make sure your url is in the video.** Yes, I know there is often a place to put your url below the video (like on YouTube). Nothing takes the place of the url showing up on the screen from time to time! There are plenty of inexpensive "post-filming" software's out there that can help you with this. Or just hire someone online at places like Fiverr.com

✓ **Make the most out of your first 15-20 seconds.** Chances are, whoever is watching your video, they are going to decide to stay or leave within that time frame. Grab them up front!

✓ **Stay focused.** Don't wander off topic. If you have another topic that you want to cover, that should be another video. A shorter video is better than one that starts rambling off topic.

Ok, I made a video...now where do I put it?

There are lots of great places to post videos...starting with your own site!

I have to assume that after reading various Be the Lime tips that you at least have your own website. If not, stop reading this and go to the website chapter NOW!

In addition to your own site, you can't overlook the elephant in the room.

YouTube

YouTube has a gazillion* videos. It is easy to use and easy to share videos. It is also, most likely, the perfect place to start when you are ready to start sharing your new creations.

If I knew something bigger than a "gazillion" I would have used that word instead.

When you open YouTube account, you are going to want to create a "Channel." A channel is pretty much like it sounds, you name it what you want and it is custom to you.

You are going to want to have similar type videos on your channel.

Your channel is your overall branding, so I would not mix personal videos and business marketing videos on the same channel.

What about videos on my own website?

Admittedly, YouTube makes it very easy to embed YouTube Videos on your WordPress website.

It is because of this that MOST people who upload videos to their channel ALSO embed the YouTube video on their own site(s).

There are really only two issues I have with using YouTube to display video on your site:

One, when you "share" a YouTube video on your site, you also (by default) share the competition's videos.

When your video is done playing, YouTube than shows "like" videos for the viewer to choose from. These might be more of your videos, they might not.

Before you know it, the person that started watching your video is off (distracted) watching a video of cats playing with a dead squirrel.

PRO TIP: You can turn off that feature, so be sure to do so if you use YouTube.

Two, there is no additional SEO benefit for your site if you are just embedding YouTube Videos.

Why not create another video (or slightly different video) and some copy, gaining you a whole new post to be seen by the world?!

I will admit, it is a bit more work to post a video directly to your site (ie: You are actually hosting the video) but there are some great video players that bolt on to WordPress and make it easier.

I like the one/two punch.

- ✓ Upload the video to YouTube and use it to drive traffic to your site.

- ✓ Host another version (or slightly different version) on your own site.

As the Buggles aptly sang, *"Video killed the radio star."*

They could have another hit if they went with, "Video killed copy."

Ok, maybe not "killed" copy, but there is no doubt a gaining popularity of people watching video online rather than reading.

You may not create a video that has a million views* but **ANY** people watching your video is a plus!

The most-watched video I created at the time of this writing has 1,083,338 views! As for my other videos...well...let's just skip those ;)

Action Items.

You know, the kind of thing Limes work on:

- Open a YouTube account.

- Create a YouTube Channel (matching your company name or focus is good).

- Make a list of topics that would be good videos.

- Make a list of questions you could answer via video.

- Think of "how" you want to shoot your video? Do you want to be on camera in a location or in front of whiteboard? Do you want to be small computer camera? What about using Power Point or ScreenFlow?

- Check out competitor's videos (if they don't have any you have a real opportunity but is there a market?).

- Download the "Recording Cheat Sheet" at BeTheLime.com/Resources

Chapter Twenty One:

NOW WHAT?

We covered a lot in this book and my goal was twofold.

First, I wanted to introduce you to some of the many tools out there that can help you increase your business and exposure - *without a lot of effort.*

You don't need another full time job; you just need to be effective.

Secondly, I wanted you to understand that you don't need to do everything.

If your business is local, Twitter probably isn't your best bet. Twitter's reach is worldwide and the conversations happen at lighting speed.

If your brand does not really have anything photo worthy, then Instagram probably is not worth your time.

If you do anything...well...Facebook and Email marketing are pretty much for everyone when used correctly.

I am going to recommend three things.

1. **Go to BeTheLime.com and sign up for the eletter.**

2. **Claim your free audio copy of Be The Lime (BeTheLime.com/LimeAudioBook)**

3. **Check out the additional resources and Cheat Sheets at BeTheLime.com/Resources**

Until next time... Be The Lime... the world has enough lemons!

Claim Your Audio Copy of
Be the Lime!

---

*"It's not true I had nothing on,
I had the radio on".*

- Marilyn Monroe

I believe we all learn in different ways.

Some of us learn reading a book, some of us learn watching a video, and some of us learn listening to audio.

Despite everyone telling me there was "no need" to include a free Audio copy of this book, I did it anyway.

Why? Because that is just the kind of things Limes do!

To claim your copy, go to

BeTheLime.com/LimeAudioBook

Also, for more audio delights...

Check out the Be the Lime Podcast on iTunes!

Resources

*"Tell me and I forget. Teach me and
I remember. Involve me and I learn."*

\- Benjamin Franklin

The biggest challenge about writing this book is that I am trying to put my foot in the same part of the river twice.

You can't. The river is moving and so is the world of online marketing.

I could list my favorite resources in this chapter and next week I would have something to add, delete, or expand upon.

It is part of why I created the **Be the Lime Monthly Membership**.

The Monthly Membership allows me to share something with members, nearly every week. Up to the minute strategies in bite sized tasks they can implement right away.

I also made the cost crazy low. Kind of a way for me to give back and help others find their way.

That said, the membership is only open to new members a couple times a year, so be sure to check it out at <u>BeTheLime.com/Membership</u> to get on the waiting list for more info.

In the interim, head over to...

BeTheLime.com/Resources

There you will find resources, cheat sheets, and an e-letter link for some fresh squeezed Lime news.

Fresh Squeezed Updates!

Get all the latest fresh squeezed Lime news at...

BeTheLime.com